KU-623-453

People & pets

A guide to choosing,
understanding and caring for your pet

Bruce Fogle

Boxtree

Contents

0727826

(m)636.088 7 f

THE COLLEGE OF WEST ANGLIA
LEARNING CENTRE

Acknowledgements

After 20 years in veterinary practice you tend to think you've seen almost everything. And so my thanks go to Granada Television and *This Morning* for allowing me to handle tarantulas, to see Toni Arthur strapped to a garden chair by an undulating 12-foot green python and to meet experts who are *passionate* about budgies and mice and guppies. My thanks as well to the viewers who rang in on the phone-ins. We naturally could only answer one in a hundred questions but I still got to see all your questions at the end of each programme and that has given me a better idea of the types of answers most wanted by pet owners. One point though. Is it possible that I noted a subdued sense of pride in your voices when you explained the curious exploits and foibles of your dogs, cats and birds?

CHAPTER 1

Why do we keep pets?

Why do we keep pets?

Here are some facts and figures. Each year we spend over two billion pounds on our pets. But what do we get in return? Buy a car or a stereo, or food, or a holiday and the return is obvious. But why on earth do so many of us spend so much money on pets?

Half of all the homes in Britain have pets. There is a dog and a cat for every ten people in the UK but surveys show that, if their circumstances allowed it, many more people would like to have pets. Although we like to think we're *the* nation of pet lovers, we actually own far fewer than many others. We need simply cross the Channel to realize that dogs in particular are everywhere in France; the French own almost twice as many as we do. Even that pales in comparison to the Australians, the world's greatest pet keepers. Down Under there are closer to three dogs for every ten people. Why do so many people burden themselves with the expense and responsibility for caring for so many animals?

Most people incorporate their pets into family photos. This is part of the Fogle family: Bruce, Liberty, Lexington and Julia.

. . . .

The burden itself can be heavy. When the director Hal Prince was rehearsing *The Phantom of the Opera* in London, he cancelled rehearsals when his dog died. One out of every three people has, at some time, to interrupt their work because of the death of a pet.

We treat pets as members of the family. We also have an unpleasant tendency to use and abuse them. But for each incident of cruelty or abuse there is often another unsung episode of care and consideration. One of my clients runs a small hotel in London in which a fire broke out recently. The guests were evacuated but, when a head count was taken, the manager realized that her Dobermann was still inside. The Fire Brigade instantly sent up a ladder to the third floor where a fireman broke in and found the unconscious dog. He carried her through the smoke and down the ladder to the waiting ambulance crew who gave her heart massage and the kiss of life. After what seemed an eternity to her owner, she coughed and spluttered. They raced her over to me and I treated her for smoke inhalation and a very sore neck - the fireman accidently dropped her as he was stepping off the ladder.

The relationship between people and pets is fascinating. It is based on the enjoyment we get from caring for them and the services, obvious or subliminal, with which they provide us. The relationship is also based on misconception. Consider my relationship with my pets.

My two golden retrievers, Lib and Lex, like the same things I like - a good tasty meal, an invigorating swim, snoozing on the floor by an open fire, a walk through the woods. They love me too. I know they love me because of the way they greet me when I walk through the front door of my house. "Oh you most wonderful person," they tell me with their eyes as they wag their backsides off the ground, grin their broadest smiles and bring me their most precious gifts - chewed nylon rings and unwashed socks. I know what they're thinking because they're so human. Or are they?

Liberty demonstrating the mouth that brings precious gifts, be they pine cones or items of unwashed laundry.

My cat is more dignified. Milly waits until the dogs have finished all their attention seeking and then comes over and insinuates herself between my legs. She's a breed called a Maine Coon so she has an awful lot of body to insinuate with. In her own refined way, she too is speaking to me. We are communicating without words. Or are we?

There is no question that of the millions of species of life that have ever existed on this earth, dogs and cats are the animals that are closest to our hearts and the ones

. . . .

Cats have more dignity. Here, Milly is communicating with an ant.

we understand best. Man's best friend has been sharing our dens, our food, our companionship and our affection for probably tens of thousands of years. Cats arrived in our homes much more recently, domesticating themselves only a few thousand years ago. They have endeared themselves to us so rapidly that they are almost as numerous as dogs. In the United States they now outnumber them.

But are pets really furry people in disguise? No animal wonders who will be the next prime minister or whether

. . . .

we will ever enter the European Monetary System or why Scotland was out in the first round of the World Cup. Of course we *know* they're not humans but somehow we still can't think of them in anything other than human terms. Although we share a surprisingly large number of likes and dislikes with them, their needs, actions and desires are sometimes different from ours.

One of the most common mistakes I hear from pet owners concerns the need of the female to have a litter. "We want her to have a litter before she's spayed so that she feels fulfilled." That feeling is only in our minds. We humans have a life-long need to nurture which is often why we keep pets. Dogs and cats don't. Their parenting instinct is programmed to last only for a matter of weeks before they come to see their pups and kits as competition rather than progeny.

Companion animals unwittingly stimulate our nurturing instinct. We instinctively respond to a baby's smiling, crying, following us, babbling, clinging, crying when we leave, lifting up the arms in greeting or clapping the hands in glee. Most of the dogs and cats I see do many of these things. Dogs especially babble with delight when they see us. They cling like glue, jump up to greet us, and look painfully sad when we leave.

And how do we show our nurturing qualities to infants? We kiss, stroke, touch and fondle them. We smile at them, cuddle and soothe them. We gaze at them and return their gibberish with our own high-pitched gibberish. And that's what I see pet owners doing with their pets every day in my reception room.

Why then do we keep pets? Is it only because they trigger our need to nurture - our need to care for living things regardless of whether they are our own children or not? Or are there other, more subtle reasons why we have so many dogs and cats? On any given date there are almost seven million cats and well over seven million dogs in the UK. Pet owning is a huge phenomenon and before going

. . . .

on to look at our relationship in more detail it is worth examining our behaviour in a general, even philosophical way.

In 1979 a group of eleven American and British doctors, veterinarians and social scientists met at the University of Dundee in Scotland to discuss some of the scientific work on people-pet relations that had been published in the 1970s, and I was one of the three veterinarians who attended. We discussed how the medical, veterinary and social science professions could work together in an interdisciplinary fashion to study the roles that pets play in society. The questions that were raised included:

1

Are pet owners different from non pet owners?

2

How do pet owners behave with their pets and why do they behave in the ways that they do?

3

Why do domestic pets behave in the way they do?

4

Are there social values in pet keeping?

5

Is there any scientific basis for the hypothesis that pets can be therapeutic in certain situations?

. . . .   **6**

What is the minimum that the veterinarian should understand about the behaviour of pet animals and the behaviour of their owners?

It was at this meeting that the term 'human-companion animal bond' was created. As far as I was concerned, the 1979 meeting was the turning point in my perception of the role of the small animal veterinarian. As a consequence of this meeting, and subsequent ones, it became apparent that in order to understand the roles pets play in our lives it is also necessary to understand why we behave the way we do with our pets. So first, a little about us.

The basis of the relationship between people and pets is attachment. Attachment is an accepted component of evolutionary behaviour and is the behaviour of the young. Its complementary behaviour in adults is nurturing. Attachment and nurturing are good for us. They keep us healthy and vital.

The American psychiatrist James Lynch, in his book, *The Broken Heart - The Medical Consequences of Loneliness*, describes how lonely people have poorer health. In a two-year study of the elderly in the farming state of Iowa, it was observed that the loneliest people were four times more likely to die than others during that period.

Other scientific studies have shown the other side of the coin: that people with good social support recover faster from congestive heart failure, from strokes or from surgery for cancer, and require less medicines to do so. Asthmatics with good social support require less steroid than those with inadequate social support. But why is this so? What is it in the evolution of the human species that has selected for greater survivability amongst those with good social support? And can companion animals play any role in alleviating loneliness and social isolation? Are pets good for our health?

Physiological research in the 1960s revealed that a dog's blood pressure drops when it is stroked. In the late 1970s it was observed that the stroker's blood pressure drops as well. (The effects of touch are not restricted to pets. Other scientific studies revealed that cows give more milk and pigs produce larger litters if they are touched, stroked, patted and talked to in a friendly way.)

By the mid 1980s other researchers had observed that simply looking at tropical fish or caged birds had a beneficial effect on the body, lowering blood pressure.

These findings are consistent with another observation which was made in the late 1970s. In a one year survival study of patients who suffered serious heart attacks, the most statistically significant factor relating to one year survival was the ownership of a pet. It didn't differ between dog and cat owners. Pet owners were more likely to survive a year after a major heart attack than non pet owners. By 1986 it was known that both heart attack prone and non heart attack prone people experience an improved cardiac response in the presence of a dog.

Aaron Katcher, a psychiatrist at the University of Pennsylvania, watched pet owners in the reception room of the University of Pennsylvania Veterinary Teaching Hospital and in their own homes. He noted that men pet their dogs and cats as much as women do. Katcher has written that pets are a culturally acceptable medium for the physical contact we instinctively need, and that pets are a means through which men can show and give affection in public.

There does, however, appear to be a striking sex difference in our attitude towards animals. Whatever the reason, culture or biology, this difference was evident in a survey I carried out recently of practising veterinarians' attitude to death in general and euthanasia in particular. One of the most striking results of the survey was the significant difference in the responses of

. . . .

men and women. Women felt much more emotional, or were willing to admit to their emotions, when pets had to be put down than men did.

In 1981, Dr Michael McCulloch, a psychiatrist in the northwest United States, published his observations on the role of pets in the treatment of emotionally ill and depressed out-patients and said that pets can be therapeutic in the following circumstances.

1

Chronic illness or disability

2

Depression

3

Role reversal and negative dependancy

4

Loneliness or isolation

5

Helplessness or hopelessness

6

Low self esteem

7

Absence of humour

. . . .

But pets can be beneficial to *all* of us, because they communicate with us in a symbolic way. Let me explain.

The sight of undisturbed animals or plants at rest is a primitive sign of safety. When I watch the rise and fall of my cat Milly's chest when she is stretched out in deep sleep, my blood pressure drops, my heart rate drops and my skin temperature drops. My state of arousal is diminished. My reaction to a gentle breeze, a storm, or a painting is primitive and biological.

But our culture affects us too. The storm wind is the symbol of danger. The sleeping watchdog is a symbol of safety. Animals at rest communicate safety.

The symbolic image of the dog is the loyal companion. A dog never grows up. We don't expect it to. We don't expect intellectual development or social concern. The pet remains subordinate, and this is most important, in a parent-child way. Aaron Katcher described the dog as a 'four-legged Peter Pan, fixed between culture and nature.' The child moves from nature to culture but the dog remains in between, neither wolf nor child. My children grow up but my pets always remain the same.

This unchanging role provides us with a constant factor in our lives. Because pets don't change, we don't have to change in our relation to them. The pet dog or cat guarantees the continuing presence of the familiar, and it is this constancy that we interpret as loyalty.

Pets communicate with us in clear and unambiguous ways. Owners, in return, often treat their pets as members of the family. In a television survey I carried out, most dog and cat owners said they allowed their pets on to their beds at least sometimes. In fact all surveys in the USA and Britain reveal that 50% of dog and cat owners let their pets sleep in the bedroom. We frequently touch our pets, occasionally celebrate their birthdays, clothe them in cold weather, talk to them, confide in them. We carry pictures of them and give

. . . .

pictures of them to their vets because the vet 'understands'. Although consciously we know it to be a fantasy, unconsciously people come to regard their pets as people. But why? What is it in our biological heritage, that makes us act this way?

The American scientific philosopher Stephen Jay Gould has lucidly argued that the history of human evolution is a history of increasing time spent nurturing infant animals. It is a reasonable hypothesis that prolonged care of infants evolved because there were deeply rooted rewards. The studies I have mentioned on the effect on your blood pressure of stroking your dog, or of loneliness on your health, are back-up for this. In other words, in the survival of the fittest, the best-nurtured passed on their genes.

We can easily understand that to be well nurtured is of paramount importance for our children. Dorothy Law said If a child lives with tolerance, he learns confidence. If he lives with praise, he learns to appreciate. If a child lives with fairness, he learns justice. If a child lives with approval, he learns to like himself, and if he lives with acceptance and friendship, he learns to find love in the world.

But just as nurturing improves survival in the young, there is now equal evidence that if we do not have the opportunity to nurture we are more prone to illness and disease. There is overwhelming evidence that social isolation, the loss of a spouse and depression lead to decreased health and increased vulnerability to accidents. Depression can be triggered by the withdrawal from the company of others and it, in turn, causes further social withdrawal. That is vastly important to remember when you consider that, by the end of the next decade, one out of every seven people in Britain will be living alone - unless they have pets.

In the course of human evolution maternal care became extended to kin care. We developed the instinctive need to care for others. Once our life-long need to nurture had developed it does not take a leap of the imagination to understand how we evolved to a stage where we could successfully rear other animals. This probably started when the young of animals killed in a hunt were brought home.

All of us in veterinary practice know from experience that playing with, feeding and caring for infant animals provide the same pleasures as nurturing human infants. Science has told us is that the emotional and physiological rewards of the two types of caring and nurturing are the same.

So it seems that caring for pets might have age old (and old age) rewards. That could explain why almost every culture in the world employs some form of pet keeping for no apparent reason other than the amusement or joy it brings. That's why so many of us do it. Throughout our history on this planet we have lived in close contact with plants and animals. But suddenly, in the last 200 years, this relationship has dramatically changed. In fact it has changed more in the last generation than ever before. Twenty-five years ago 80% of vets looked after livestock. Today 80% of us look after pets. And as we have become an urban species, dogs and cats have become an important vestige of our former bond with the natural world, a physiological bond that evolved over countless generations. We cling to these vestiges because nurturing makes us feel better and contributes to our good health.

However, in clinging to dogs and cats in the way we do, we can lose sight of the reason for our behaviour and in doing so destroy their status as real animals and make them instead into degraded images of humans.

And to complicate matters even more, because pets have no obvious material value, their purpose is only dictated through their social relationship with us. That's why pets can be loved like children and yet still be discarded like rags. This too is the reason why there is such an

Playing with pets is good for our well-being. It's good for theirs too.

enormous variation in our social and cultural responses to them.

These are the reasons why we almost instinctively want to come into a closer relationship with animals. It is a part of human nature, but our response to this universal feeling will vary according to our cultural traditions. The Western tradition, in which man had dominion over all of nature, has been perhaps more readily able than other cultures to evolve to a state where we are now saying that we have a responsibility for all nature. We are coming to a better appreciation of the behaviour of people and pets. After all, to understand the world around us we must first understand ourselves.

What we are creating today in our revitalized interest in all animals, although we might not yet realize that we are doing so, is a profoundly new relationship with the natural world. The social and psychological value of animals, and this for many people in the industrialized world means dogs and cats, outweigh their material worth. Their value lies in the relationship between them and us. That's what I'll discuss in the next chapters.

CHAPTER 2

Our relationship with pets

Our relationship with pets

● The Emotional Relationship

In 1980, the first international meeting on people-pet relations was held in London. Further international meetings have been held approximately every three years with the most recent in Monaco in November 1989.

One of the speakers at that meeting was Lionel Tiger who described the evolution of our relationship with animals and nature. Briefly, he explained that when we were hunters, our relationship to animals was one to one. "Every hunter was his own ethologist," he said.

With agriculture came a change in our relationship with animals. Farmers had to understand their animals in order for them to be successful farmers. "Every farmer was his own ethologist."

But, with the industrial age, animals became redundant to most of us. Tiger says that, today, our keeping of plants in our homes is a way of 'importing' our past relationship with nature into our lives. The same is true of pets - animals that he calls 'ambassadors' from the past.

Some say that our interest in pets - animals with no economic value or function - might indicate a willingness on our part to act unselfishly. Others say that when parents buy pets for their children they are really saying how important or pleasurable it is to be a parent. After all, children and pets require attention, energy, resources. You could even say that both are unnecessary luxuries.

The more scientific argue that there are practical reasons why we have developed such a strong emotional bond with pets. The late Nobel Prize winner Professor Konrad Lorenz was the first to suggest that the shape of the infant's head - with its large forehead, short face and protruding cheeks release instinctive parental behaviour in us.

Of course it isn't only Nobel Prize winners who make such discoveries. Walt Disney was just as observant and doll makers too have learned that by creating 'superimages' or 'superbaby' features they can produce characters that are often sweeter than the real things. Just think of Bambi. This is in fact what we have unconsciously done through selective dog and cat breeding.

To create the pets we have today, we've modified two species, dogs and cats, so that their juvenile or babyish behaviour is perpetuated through life. And through selective breeding we've also created pets that act as 'superstimuli', bringing out the parent in us - pets with big innocent eyes and helpless looks.

Scientists have explained how important touch is to our well-being. It isn't just being touched that is good for us. To be denied the chance to touch can have disastrous effects on our health. Working from this base of knowledge, scientists in the late 1970s and throughout the 1980s began looking at what possible benefits pets might bring to families and individuals. As everything needs a title, the research was called Pet Therapy and the table on page 24 shows some of the circumstances in which doctors, psychiatrists and psychologists have recommended Pet Therapy in the United States.

A popular fallacy is that the elderly are the loneliest group, but adolescence is the phase of life when loneliness looms largest. Loneliness is associated with widowhood, but marriage is no guarantee of avoiding loneliness.

In veterinary practice I see more women than men (a nice perk). I also see more affection between women and their pets than between men and their dogs or cats. Women are more likely than men to acknowledge they are lonely and are more likely to show affection in

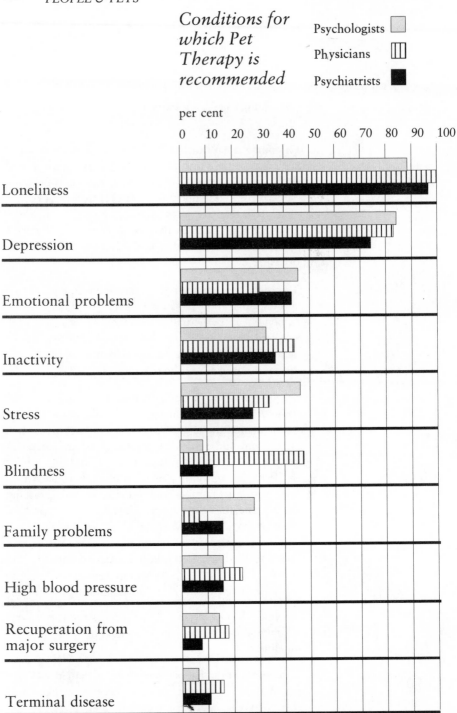

Conditions for which Pet Therapy is recommended

Psychologists
Physicians
Psychiatrists

per cent

0 10 20 30 40 50 60 70 80 90 100

Loneliness

Depression

Emotional problems

Inactivity

Stress

Blindness

Family problems

High blood pressure

Recuperation from major surgery

Terminal disease

24

As you can see, almost 100% have recommended pets for people who are lonely.

public. But when more subtle measures of loneliness are used, men often have higher scores than women. Men sometimes have a greater emotional dependence on their pets, of which they are unaware until the relationship is threatened. And when a threat comes, men can behave in far more dramatic ways than women do. In these emotionally fraught circumstances I find that the wives are almost always better at handling situations than are their husbands.

Emotional loneliness is more painful than social loneliness and probably occurs in men more commonly than in women. And in these circumstances, pets can be a two-edged sword. For those people without fellow humans to care for or be cared for by, a pet can be a marvellous escape from loneliness. But for some other people it can also become an emotional crutch, an outlet for the affection which they can't give to other humans. All vets in practice meet people like this - often men, and often female cat 'collectors' too. These people will sacrifice their social bonds with people in order to retain their emotional bonds with their four-legged companions.

The opposite side of the equation is what I see most, and is probably what makes veterinary practice so enjoyable. There is a great deal of evidence to show that keeping active enhances our moods and that happy people are rarely lonely. In American surveys of what people enjoy most about their pets, the consistent answer is, "He makes me laugh." Pets are funny.Few mean to be but they are. Their very seriousness is amusing: Lib bringing me my kid's dirty socks; Milly, in the middle of frenetic play, suddenly breaking off to race through the living room, dining room, kitchen and hallway to her litterbox in the back room. We enjoy their behaviour because it is so patently honest and real and uncomplicated.

. . . .

There are a few simple reasons why this is so. Just like infants, pets are 'pre-verbal'. And because of that there is never any chance of a verbal misunderstanding. Dogs in particular, but also cats raised in human contact from an early age, enjoy physical contact with us. Most people also crave closeness. Pets offer unconditional affection - something that is virtually unattainable from fellow humans. In a nutshell, pets provide emotional security for those who need it, and most of us do.

I'm not saying that only pets offer emotional security. Far from it. Parents should provide it for children and, in the natural evolution of life, children should provide it for their parents. Couples provide it for each other. So do friends. But life doesn't always follow the rules we would like it to. According to speakers at the Monaco meeting, over half of all New Yorkers live alone. An even larger percentage of the inhabitants of Norway live alone. Loneliness is a fact of life today - exaggerated by increasing impersonal urbanization. Together with a feeling of lack of security, that's one of the reasons why the number of urban pets is increasing so dramatically.

Dogs make us smile, especially smiling dogs.

The potential for the emotional relationship we have with our pets has always been there. But it is only as our society changes that the potential is being realized. With the disintegration of the three-generation family and the reduction of the importance of religion, some of the former glues of society, which cemented the emotional basis of our lives, have been dissolved. Aspects of security, things we could turn to, are no longer there. Pets fill this emotional void, contented to be 'used' by us in a new way because there's something in it for them. Dogs in particular are being used in dramatically new and exciting ways.

● *The Practical Relationship*

Pets give and receive affection. They also give us something to do. We talk to them, take them for exercise and play with them. Dogs protect us and our homes, or at least we like to think they do. But in sheer practical terms they are taking on new and rewarding roles. Cats have become resident mascots in old folks homes and even in prisons. Dogs are taken into hospitals to cheer up patients. Some are trained to help the deaf or blind, others to detect drugs at airports or even fungus infestations in lumber yards. They are trained to help the disabled, to rescue people from the sea, to find victims of earthquake, avalanche or other disaster, and in standard police work and search and rescue. Dogs are being trained to serve us in more ways than ever before.

For centuries man has admired, enjoyed and sometimes exploited the loyalty, intelligence and strength of dogs. The dog was the first species that we domesticated and has always been considered man's best friend. He was used to guard our homes, to protect our livestock, to carry our burdens and to hunt our game. By the nineteenth century, British dogs in particular excelled at working, hunting and retrieving. Their descendants still behave in these specific ways which is why my golden retrievers are always retrieving embarrassing things, when guests arrive (but with such panache and enjoyment that its difficult to get angry at them).

The world has changed dramatically since these breeds evolved, but just when it seemed that working dogs would forever be consigned to retrieving dirty socks, their duties have been channelled into new and exciting roles.

In Tokyo, an elderly woman takes her pet bird for a walk.

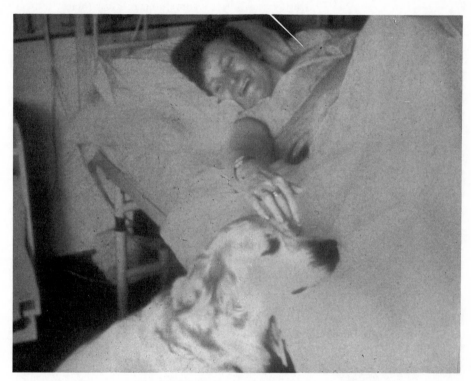

Pets can bring cheer in the most difficult circumstances.

The oldest 'new' role is to act as eyes for blind individuals. Guide Dogs for the Blind came into being around 1930 and is now the world's largest dog breeding organization. Here in Britain the new guide dog is a labrador - golden retriever cross. In other countries the German shepherd is still more frequently used. In Australia, the local guide dog association has successfully experimented with adding a dollop of standard poodle to their retriever mix, to produce an intelligent and responsive dog that doesn't shed as much as retrievers do, and so might be a better companion for an allergic blind person.

Dogs that helped the blind have been written about since at least the time of Christ, but it is only in the last 50 years that this practical application has been seriously tested and used. Pups from the association's 250 breeding bitches are born in selected private homes and then at around six weeks of age they're moved into other family homes where they are taught basic obedience and standard commands. At about one year of age, they leave these homes and undergo seven to nine months basic training at one of the six regional training centres. They then go on to more advanced work like 'no sniffing on the job'. 'On the job' means whilst in harness. (This is where my golden sniffers would probably fail.) Training finishes with a month's training with the new owner.

Newfoundland dogs are trained in France for sea rescue.

The physical function of the guide dog is obvious but there is a psychological and social value too. Research here in Britain revealed that owners of guide dogs feel they are the elite amongst the blind. Further detailed research in the United States revealed that, rather than feeling dependent on their dogs, blind owners feel interdependent. Just as the blind person needs the dog to act as eyes for him, the dog needs the blind person to regulate and reinforce his training, to reward work well done, to feed him, groom him, exercise him, play with him or just talk with him. guide dogs need affection, attention and protection from the stresses of work - all provided by their owners. The result is true interdependence which boosts the self esteem of the owner.

I was aware of this research when the charity Hearing Dogs for the Deaf was set up. I had better explain that I have a vested interest in this organization as I have been involved from the outset.

Having seen the value and success of Guide Dogs, Hearing Dogs was set up to find, train and place a good set of canine 'ears' in the homes of profoundly deaf people.

Deafness is an invisible loss. If you meet a blind person you might help him cross the road; if you meet a deaf person you're more likely to shout at him. The consequence is that the deaf carry a collective chip on the shoulder because the 'hearing world' doesn't appreciate how catastrophic the loss can be. When people who have lost both sight and hearing are asked which sense they miss most, almost half say hearing.

Hearing dogs are completely different to guide dogs. They are the antithesis of the perfectly bred dog and a classic example of practical recycling. Hearing dogs are rejects - not very pretty but superbright and alert young dogs. Most are rescued, either as young 'teenagers' around a year of age or as unwanted pups. If they are young pups they go through a socialization period, as do guide dogs, in private homes. Older dogs are selected from animal rescue associations such as The Canine Defence League, Wood Green Animal Shelters and the Blue Cross. They are taken to the purpose-built Hearing Dog Training Centre at Lewknor, Oxfordshire,where they undergo three months of training to first verbal and then visual commands.

Each dog is trained to alert his owner to several specific noises such as the doorbell, the alarm clock and the telephone. Specific training for the intended recipient then follows. If, for example, a deaf mother wants her hearing dog to tell her when the baby is crying, then this is added to the training schedule. At the end of the three months, the recipient comes to the training centre for a week of training with her new set of 'ears'. The first 100 dogs are out working now and, with recent expansion of kennel facilities, the number of graduates will increase in 1991 to 40 per year. In the near future, funds permitting, a second training centre will be built to help meet demand.

As with guide dogs, the physical function of hearing dogs is obvious but the less obvious values are equally important. In surveys, 79% of pet owners say their pets understand how they feel. Deaf people feel the same about their hearing dogs, and the consequence is mute communication. It's overwhelmingly frustrating to be deaf, as I've been told by countless hearing dog owners. But if you feel your pet understands your frustration, that eases the burden just a little.

Easing the burden even more are the over 4,700 registered PAT dogs in Britain. These are regularly taken into hospitals, old folks homes and other institutions to break the monotony and add a little happiness to the lives of those who find themselves 'institutionalized'.

An American professor has described old folks homes this way: "Loneliness, depression, hopelessness, helplessness, boredom and low self-esteem are

. . . .

characteristics shared by many residents in custodial institutions, particularly in those catering to the aged." Many old folks homes are highly regimented, leaving little room for individuality. People can lose their sense of purpose, the feeling of being loved or of giving love. And then in comes a smiling, slobbering English setter. The presence of a benign animal, willing to be stroked, *asking* to be stroked, can't help but break the monotony of life. The weekly or twice weekly visits give residents

Hearing dogs for the deaf are trained to act as ears for profoundly deaf people.

. . . .

something to look forward to, and make them feel just that little bit better.

Many institutions, especially in Scotland, have taken this concept one step farther and actually 'employ' resident mascots. Sedentary and rather slothful cats are particularly suitable; the ideal institution pet is one that is free, of course, from disease, small enough to be placed on a bed and willing to stay there for extended periods of time.

New practical uses of our relationship with pets are more dramatically demonstrated by scenting dogs such as Customs and Excise drug detectors, Police and RAF explosives detectors and the fungus in the woodpile detectors. In France, special units of earthquake and avalanche rescue dogs are always available for deployment in France or abroad. They were amongst the first rescuers at the scene of the Armenian earthquake in 1988. Unfortunately, the strict Muslim cultural laws vetoed their use after the Iranian earthquake in the summer of 1990. In Britain the same rescue role is performed by the various search and rescue dog associations (SARDA).

PAT dogs make regular visits to old folks homes, bringing warmth to lonely lives.

· Last year my family and I attended the four day SARDA dog and dog handler assessment in the Lake District. I was 'planted' in the hills and eventually rescued by Sam, a four-year-old border collie. Just as the police have discovered that springer spaniels make good scent detectors because they get so excited, SARDA has discovered that border collies make good search and rescue dogs because they latch onto air scent and don't get distracted. All of them are family pets and none has a nose for sheep. In that sense, they are classic examples of new recycling of old models. Because they are not interested in sheep, they are useless to shepherds as sheep dogs, but they are ideal to be trained to search for lost walkers in sheep-laden country.

Dogs are being trained for other new roles. Whilst in Monaco I saw demonstrations of sea rescue dogs - massive Newfoundlands that jump out of helicopters and pull dinghies or wind surfing boards in to safety. The dogs were magnificent and obviously enjoyed their

The dogs sensitive sense of smell makes it an ideal rescue aid at the sight of avalanches.

. . . .

work, but I couldn't help wondering what it was all for. If the helicopter is already hovering overhead, why ask the dog to go for a swim?

Training dogs to help disabled people has more merit. This has been done in the United States for over a decade and is just starting here. In its simplest form, the dog, usually an affable large dog like a retriever, is trained to help its wheelchair-bound owner. If the owner drops something, the dog picks it up and gives it to his owner. If the owner has difficulty getting the wheelchair up a curb, the dog adds his strength by pulling. If the owner can't reach the 'up' button for the lift, the dog is trained to stand on his hind legs and push the button.

But just as with guide dogs and hearing dogs, the greatest rewards from assistance dogs are the subtle ones. In one experiment, some people restricted to their wheelchairs followed a set route along some Berkeley, California, streets whilst observers marked down how many interactions occurred with people. The same people then followed the same route but this time with their assistance dogs dressed in their fluorescent backpacks. The number of interactions soared. People stopped to say 'hello' to the dogs and then to their owners. Others asked to help the disabled people up and down curbs. The dogs were social ice-breakers, slicing through the inhibitions we have whenever we see anyone that is not quite like the rest of us.

Our practical relationship with animals is important although not always obvious. And anecdote is important. The fact that all societies and cultures incorporate animal anecdote into their myths and legends tells us how important it is. These stories tell us why animals are important to people and those of us in clinical practice hear them every day.

"She's part of the family."

"He gives me something to do."

"She gives me responsibility."

. . . .

The fact that stroking your cat lowers your blood pressure or causes you to release endorphins in your brain is scientifically interesting but there is more than science to the changing relationship we have with animals. The fact is that farmers talk to their cows, cowboys talk to their horses and pet owners talk to their dogs and cats. It's something that virtually defies scientific investigation. Talking to animals doesn't mean that they understand what we're saying or that we even expect them to but rather it's another way we have of touching animals and nurturing them. We touch them with our thoughts and pat them with our voices.

One of the problems in observing how we interact with our pets is that the relationship is so familiar we have lost our ability to describe it analytically. How do you

scientifically describe a 'warm' conversation between a pet owner and a pet? The American humorist James Thurber said that he thought that a 'dog lover' was a dog in love with another dog! More scientifically, Dr Kenneth Keddie, a psychiatrist from Scotland, has written that, "Animals bolster the pet owner's morale and remind him that he is, in fact, a special and unique individual."

In the *American Journal of Psychiatry*, Dr A Seigal, a psychiatrist from New England wrote, "The animal does not judge but offers a feeling of intense loyalty; it does not expose

The value of animals crosses continents.

its master to the ugly strain of constant criticism. It provides its owner with a chance to feel important." The American anthropologist Margaret Mead once wrote, "One of the oldest human needs is having someone wonder where you are when you don't come home at night."

Behavioural experiments on many different species of animal have shown that mammals and birds are capable of understanding the world and of representing it symbolically in their heads. The language experiments with chimpanzees and gorillas in which these animals learned American sign language did not prove that animals have language. But they did prove that animals can think in sentences. Washoe, the first chimp to be taught sign language, learned 132 different signs and invented new ones. Jane Goodall tells the story of Lucy, raised in a human household at the University of Oklahoma and sent, after ten years, to a chimpanzee reserve in the Gambia in Africa. When, two years later, someone from her former life visited the reserve, Lucy ran to the fence of her enclosure and signed, 'Please. Help. Out.'

It is not only primates that have this ability. Richard Herrnstein, working at Harvard University in Boston, trained pigeons to peck at a panel when they saw a tree projected on a screen. They continued to peck at the panel when shown pictures of different shaped trees, or trees in the foreground or the background of pictures or even in silhouette. So pigeons can form categories for things in their brains. Imagine what mammals like dogs and cats can do.

We shouldn't take our pets for granted. They really are 'human' in that they have emotions and feelings similar to ours. Scientists as eminent as Konrad Lorenz have observed that, for example, jealous behaviour in birds has the same function as jealous behaviour primates, including us. Our pets are not simply pre-wired machines

. . . . following their instincts. Each is a unique individual, yet we unfortunately tend to forget it.

● *The Unpleasant Relationship*

There are two negative aspects of our relationship with dogs and cats. The first concerns the fact that they are abused and abandoned. The second concerns a lack of social responsibility on the part of their owners. It is the latter that leads to serious dog bites and the fouling of gardens, pavements and parks.

Pet abuse is common. You need only ring The Cat's Protection League or Wood Green Animal Shelters to discover the size of the problem. Cats are used for target practice with air rifles. Dogs are beaten and starved. I see little of this abuse because I'm in private practice. Pet owners pay for the services I provide and animal abusers certainly aren't going to do that. But even so I recently treated a garrulous, outgoing, smiling and friendly young dog for his injuries suffered in a road traffic accident. It seemed like a typical accident until I was told that some teenagers had held the dog on one side of the road, waited for a car to come alone and then had their friends on the other side of the road call the dog. They had set up the accident, taking advantage of the dog's innocent belief that humans are good.

The RSPCA and its sister associations in Scotland and Ulster are confronted with stories such as this on a daily basis. Abused and abandoned pets are a national disgrace - a problem we try to pretend doesn't exist. Fortunately, a minority of pet owners indulge in cruelty, but bites and faeces are two common aspects of our relationship with pets that should concern all of us.

● *Bites*

Dogs and cats bite. It's natural. They're carnivores. They bite when they're frightened or in pain or when they're too young to understand how hard they are biting. In all of these situations biting is understandable. But it's not understandable or acceptable when pets bite because they have not been properly trained to inhibit their biting or when they have been actively trained to bite.

Adult cats bite when frightened or, curiously, when they have been stroked too much. Their bites are not usually terribly serious although they can lead to infection if not properly treated. Dog bites however can be lethal.

Hospital statistics show that large dogs are the worst offenders, but these statistics are misleading as only the worst bites need hospital treatment. In his survey of 56 breeds of dogs, Dr Benjamin Hart, in *The Perfect Puppy*, reported that as far as biting potential was concerned, breeds such as the golden retriever and Hungarian Viszla were amongst the least likely to bite (scoring one on his chart), breeds such as Dobermanns, German shepherds and Rottweilers were middling in their tendency to bite (scoring five on his chart) whilst terriers such as westies, yorkies and wire-haired fox terriers were the most likely to bite (scoring ten on the chart).

Animal behaviourists such as Roger Mugford and Peter Neville say that 70% of the cases they see involve aggression, but there are different types of aggression. In Mugford's statistics, the labradors he saw tried to bite other male dogs but not humans, whereas the cocker spaniels tried to bite humans not dogs and the nervous German shepherds tried to bite both. But can our relationship with dogs produce animals that bite?

The most troublesome breed of dog today is the American pit bull terrier, followed some distance behind by the Rottweiler. In North America more human deaths and serious injuries are caused by this breed than by any other. They have been selectively bred to attack and to hold on tenaciously. Their jaw muscles can be inches thick with a crushing power of hundreds of pounds per square inch. All the information that there is on the breed points to the fact that these dogs are killing machines. Yet I now see dozens of them, owned by my clients, and have not as yet seen a dog-to-dog dispute in my reception room between one of these and another dog (yet I often see that with male Cavalier King Charles spaniels of all breeds).

When 20 human fatalities from pit bull terrier attacks in the United States were studied, several common facts were noted. Ten of the 20 lethal dogs were owned by young men between 20 and 25 years old. Eleven of the 20 owners had criminal records. Seven of the 20 owners had criminal records for violence. Eleven of the 20 dogs showed signs of physical abuse.

I'm not recommending pit bulls as pets. There is no question that the pit bull terrier has been selectively bred for heightened and tenacious aggression. Similarly, in the selective breeding to produce the Rottweiler, a temperamental defect whereby the dog goes from relaxed to aggressive without warning has unfortunately crept into the breed. But the problem is not simply one of genetics. It is a problem based on the relationship that some people, especially young men, have with their dogs, where the dog is encouraged to be a weapon rather than simply a companion. I don't see problem pit bulls because they come from secure homes with two adults and 2.3 kids and are taken to a private vet for care and attention. They are treated as members of the family.

● *Faeces*

An equally unpleasant aspect of our relationship with pets involves their sanitary habits. When we moved to our new home a few years ago, it only took a day to realize that the local tom cat was using our back garden as his lavatory, and small dogs were being allowed to defecate on the pavement outside the front gate of the house. Always right outside the gate, in the most annoying place possible.

Some people are simply irresponsible and give all dog owners a bad name. But most local authorities don't help by failing to place dog dirt bins in places where residents walk their dogs.

In Monaco, self-explanatory signs encourage responsible pet ownership.

Cat faeces is an aesthetic as well as a health problem. Although it is rare, some cats can transmit a disease called Toxoplasmosis which is dangerous to the unborn child of pregnant women. Around 30% of the population host this organism. Most have picked it up by eating undercooked meat, but infection can also occur through contact with cat faeces.

If a woman cat owner is pregnant or planning to become pregnant she should do two things. The first is simply have a blood test for Toxoplasmosis. If positive, she has

. . . .

been exposed to the organism and has produced protection against it.

If she is negative however, she should have her cat tested by a vet for Toxo and, to be completely safe, use washing up gloves when she cleans the litter tray. And, of course, stick to well-cooked meat whilst pregnant as uncooked or undercooked meat is the most common source of Toxoplasmosis.

Dog faeces is also an aesthetic and health problem and we can easily do something about both. The health aspect concerns the dog roundworm, toxocara canis. Around 40 years ago it was discovered that this parasite is a potential health hazard to humans. But for us to be infected we need three factors: a young dog passing toxocara eggs in the faeces, a suitable environment in which these eggs can incubate for several weeks and a person liable to ingest the dirt.

Owning a cat is perfectly safe if a few simple rules are followed.

Toxocara can be controlled through two methods: correct worming of our dogs and cleaning up their mess so that eggs don't have a chance to incubate.

Discoveries about Toxocara in dogs are still being made and, as these discoveries occur, worming recommendations change. In the past few years new wormers have been developed that are infinitely better than those that were available even a few years ago. These new wormers kill not only the adult worms in dogs that have them, but also the microscopic larval stages that were not destroyed by old wormers.

Bitches are more likely to pass roundworms than dogs, either when they are pregnant or after each season. The rule of thumb then is to worm pregnant bitches effectively, to worm pups and then to worm your dog twice yearly. Bitches effectively should also be wormed after each season. To be absolutely safe, the ideal arrangement is to worm your dog every three months with the new types of wormers available from your vet.

Cleaning up after your dog can be more difficult.

Westminster, which is where my veterinary practice is, has one of the most logical, well thought-out initiatives to promote responsible pet ownership. Westminster has set up the City of Westminster Dog Owner's Club. Members get special tags for their dogs and qualify for reductions on such veterinary treatments as vaccinations, worming and neutering operations from all the vets in Westminster.

The City set up signs outside areas where residents walk their dogs saying, 'Its fun to own a dog in Westminster', made poop scoops available cheaply and easily from all Council outlets and installed dog dirt bins in the parks, open spaces and housing estates run by the Council. Special exercise areas were set aside for dog owners and free dog training classes arranged for all members of the dog club.

. . . .

Having set up this good, sensible infrastructure there was now no excuse for dog owners *not* to clean up after their dogs. And if people didn't, the Council introduced new byelaws to upgrade enforcement, and give it some 'bite', if you'll pardon the expression.

The health problem of dog faeces is minimal but the aesthetic problem is considerable. It's simply unpleasant to step in dog muck or worse to sit in it in the park. As our relationship with our pets continues to evolve, the aesthetic aspect becomes more and more important. This is something over which we have complete control if only we choose to use it.

CHAPTER 3

The roles of pets through our lives

The roles of pets through our lives

Pets play different roles and serve different purposes throughout our lives. Advertisers use the fact that animals have a subconscious effect on us, to sell products as varied as beer, cars, toilet tissue, coal and paint. According to research that was presented in Monaco, cats are associated in our minds with cleanliness, quiet and speed whilst dogs suggest faithfulness, fidelity and sympathy. Cats have 'female' values according to advertisers, and are associated with adjectives such as soft, warm, beautiful, capricious and elegant. Dogs have 'male' values and are associated with words such as strong, fast, companion and outdoors.

I see pets as being a window into the attitudes and behaviour of the family in which they live. Both the social services and the RSPCA know that abused pets come out of homes where there are abused children. The way a pet is treated, its name, the way it is groomed and fed - all these things tell me something about the family it lives with. You might say that its none of my business to know what the family is like but, from a clinical perspective, it helps me make an accurate diagnosis and is one of the most important facts that a vet can use.

Babies don't need pets. They're of no value to infants and crawlers and just get in the way. For the first six months of life an infant can't differentiate between himself, his mother, his father and his surroundings. He can't make a distinction between something living like a cat and something inanimate like a toy. But if you already have a pet and want to introduce it to the new baby there are some simple rules to follow.

1

Dogs and cats are curious animals. Don't isolate them from the baby or discipline their curiosity.

2

Allow them to see and smell the baby when the baby is sleeping.

3

Combine the sight and smell of the baby with something positive that your pet enjoys, like a pat or a titbit.

4

Play with your dog or cat to let it know you're still just as interested in him.

5

Try to keep to his old routine as much as possible.

6

Never leave your baby and your pet alone together.

That last point is important. Most of us forget the origins of our pets. We should think of them as hunters until we are satisfied that there will be no problems.

Children as young as three and a half years can show maternal care towards pets. But even at this early age their behaviour has been modified by what they have seen and even by the stories they have been told. Studies of animals in children's literature show that in many cases books blur the distinction between pets and people. Pets speak, or drive cars or in other ways act like us. Also, books portray animals as being more tolerant of handling, less aggressive and more forgiving than they are in real life.

The other side of the coin is that, in giving animals human emotions, we are teaching children that animals *do* have emotions. This is surely important if we are to improve their general welfare.

During childhood pets become fun. The active dog or cat is amusing and helps the child to develop his basic

Children are uninhibited about having fun with pets.

abilities. (It also probably has more energy than the mother or father and can actually take some of the 'child minding' responsibility by playing with the child.)

Some psychiatrists call pets 'transitional objects' - direct descendants from the satin-edged blanket and the soft stuffed toy. These things allow the child to feel safe, secure and active without the parents being present.

Ten years of age is probably the youngest that a child can be responsible for a pet. Psychologists say that when children are this age, a pet can become a real companion or confidant. They offer emotional support and teach children about friendliness and caring. In some circumstances they can also teach about toilet training, sexual behaviour, pregnancy, birth and the inevitable death of all living things.

Pets are great fun for kids but until they are old enough to care for an animal genuinely it's important that parents take on that responsibility and teach their children the following simple rules.

1

Never approach strange animals.

2

Never put your face near an animal's teeth or claws.

3

Be wary of dogs that are raised in homes without children.

4

Be careful when entering a house with a dog.

Dogs and cats are considered part of the family - not quite human, but still not quite as 'animal' as all other animals.

Left, Bill, a Macaw, trying to remove my son Ben's school uniform.

Right, Humphrey, our African Grey parrot spends the evening on the window shouting greetings to passers-by.

Right, dogs love licking faces, definitely not a habit to encourage.

Opposite, looks can be deceiving. Gentle pups can grow up to become tearaways if they aren't handled properly when very young.

Above and left, Julia and the dogs are always pretty as a picture.

Below, my daughter Tamara, Milly, Liberty and Lexington watching the World cup.

5

Never try to stop two animals from fighting even if one is your own.

6

Never disturb an animal that is eating or sleeping.

7

Never carry your food near an animal.

8

Learn the danger signals that animals give when they are alarmed or angry.

Parents should also do the following with their children.

1

Supervise a child when he meets new animals.

2

Supervise a child when he is learning to feed an animal.

3

Supervise a child when he is learning to exercise an animal.

4

Do not let small children exercise large dogs.

Growing up is a serious business, even when shared.

Adolescence has its ups and downs. According to some research from the University of California, adolescents share 'secrets' with their pets in much the same way they do with their grandparents. And teenagers who share 'secrets' with their pets and their grandparents are more likely to have greater empathy with their own age group.

Pets can be fulfilling or a nuisance for teenagers. For my children they are the former. My son is away at school, happy to be away but for the fact that he is separated from his dogs. My younger daughter is addicted to Milly the Maine Coon and watches her for hours - something, incidentally that is exceptionally easy to do and a fine way of avoiding homework.

Because animals are subordinate, they are always vulnerable to redirected aggression. Adolescence is the age of experimention for boys, influenced by their recently discovered male hormones, and pets can take the brunt of that experimenting.

Animals are tormented in almost every society and adolescent boys are those most likely to do the tormenting. As I've mentioned, tormenting is a natural stage that

· ·

many boys go through but it can persist in boys who need to display dominance or who need to score points with their friends. Persistent cruelty to animals during adolescence is a strong predictor that a boy will have a future of violence.

Fortunately, adolescents grow up. And this is the time of life when a pet is of least value. Pets tie you down at the one time of your life when you have the freedom to spread your wings. But even at this stage of life I still see many pet owners, usually young women who have moved to London, are living alone and want the companionship of an animal, usually a cat.

Cats are excellent companions for working women. If kittens are raised to expect nothing but their own curiosity to amuse themselves during the day, they grow up to spend their sleeping hours during the day alone and then to play with their owners during the evening.

Cats are marvellous at entertaining themselves.

. . . .

Young men who have pets during this phase of their lives often have big dogs, to enhance the image they want to portray.

When image becomes important, pets can take on the role of status symbols. Creating an identity helps the young adult position himself where he wants to be. Right now old-fashioned dogs like Jack Russell terriers or wire-haired fox terriers are the correct image for the trendiest of young Londoners.

Pets have always been used as status symbols but today over 350,000 pedigree pups are registered with the Kennel Club each year and almost 35,000 pedigree kittens with the Governing Council of the Cat Fancy. Over 60% of dogs and 10% of cats in Britain are pedigree, the largest numbers ever. When I bought Milly recently my clients just assumed it was a pedigree but what surprised me was how many actually knew what a Maine Coon was. (It's a big New England alley cat with a gentle disposition and proper no knots long hair.)

When young men and women get pets at this stage in their lives, they are making a statement. They're saying that they're the settling down types and are happy to look after a family. Marriage may come along. But today many married couples are putting off having children so that both husband and wife can continue to work.

The image of the pet is that it belongs to a nuclear family: a husband, wife, a few children and a dog or cat. In my practice nuclear families are in a minority. Single parent families, childless couples, homosexual couples, parents whose children have left home, all form a larger percentage of the people I see than families such as my own.

Scientific studies have shown that pet ownership is highest among young people who have formed permanent relationships, whether they are married or not. But in those relationships where having children is

. . . . postponed, pets play a more important role. Childless couples interact and play with their dogs and cats much more than couples with children. The dogs incidentally are always monitoring their owner's availability and spend more time near their childless owners than do dogs that are owned by families with children. Childless couples interrupt what they are doing to talk to or touch their pets on average five times per hour, whilst couples with children only talk to or touch their pets on average twice an hour.

The classic image of the pet is that of the member of the nuclear family. Virtually every estate car manufacturer has used that image at one time or another in promoting their products as family vehicles. Dogs and cats *are* members of the family and are treated like children, housed and fed well, taken to the vet when they are unwell and either taken on holidays with the family or installed in kennels. Boarding a dog or cat is not necessarily as traumatic for them as it sometimes is for you. For dogs in particular, boarding can actually be stimulating - an exciting break from an otherwise boring routine of eat - sleep - eat.

Parents think their children will 'learn' from animals; learn things like responsibility and friendship, love and respect. Parents often tell me they've bought the pet for their children, but in fact it's often for themselves.

Pets may seem to be child substitutes but symbolically they are also parent substitutes. They provide things that our parents provided when we were babies: security, contact comfort, warmth and unending 'superabundant' love. Sure, we speak to our pets in what linguists call 'motherese', the language mothers use when they speak to their babies. But we get rewards that only parents can give - safety, fidelity, loyalty and a kind of unalloyed affection that only exists in a fantasy world of make believe.

As the children grow up their parent's relationship with pets can change. When I lived with my parents the house

. . . . was filled with everything that could creep, crawl, slither, walk, swim and fly. My father acquired them, and my mother looked after them. Today, when I visit my parents, it's my father who looks after the dog, walks her, feeds her and, in the heat of the Florida sun, picks fleas off her! What happened was that as the children left home my parents' routines changed. And as they did, the dog became more important because it was still there. That's not always possible because as families break up the parents often move to smaller homes where there can be restrictions on keeping pets.   Ironically, these restrictions are most common on council estates where, because of social isolation, the need for companionship is very often the greatest.

When children leave home, pets can take on the role of care receivers. And nurturing is good for us.

. . . . A few years ago in the United States the law was changed: it became permissible for the elderly to take their pet dogs and cats with them if they moved into public housing. After this legislation had been in place for some time, the consequences were examined by a team from the University of California. They surveyed the managers of all the housing authorities in California that were affected by this legislation, as well as residents who didn't own pets. Most of the managers and most of the non pet owners favoured the legislation even though negative opinions were sought. A majority of people volunteered that problems were fewer than expected. The most common problem was stray cats and some consequent results such as disturbed flower beds. And needless to say, the pet owners themselves were overwhelmingly happy that they could keep their companions.

When doctors have studied ageing they have asked a simple question: "What are the main predictors of happiness in old age?" The answers are, having a partner with whom you are relaxed and with whom you can confide, having a partner in good health, physical activity and your perception of your own health as good. At the Monaco meeting a further report was presented on the role pets might play in promoting happiness in old age. In this study, pet owners reported having a larger number of friends and were more likely to belong to an organized group than non pet owners.

In both physical and psychological tests, pet owners were fitter than non pet owners. Of course, there is the question of cause and effect. Are these people in better condition because they have pets, or are they in good condition and - as a consequence - have pets. Either way, it confirms the impression that I have from practice that pet owners are more active, more sociable and friendlier than people who actively say they don't like pets.

The elderly are the fastest growing segment of the

Pets can bring happiness at all stages of life.

population and I can see the day when I reach that classification. The fact that we have failed to care for our elderly properly is mirrored in the World Health Organization report revealing that the elderly in Third World countries often live fuller lives and have higher social status than the elderly of the richer, industrialized countries. It shouldn't be left to pets to comfort them in their old age. Pets should augment rather than replace the care and attention that our old people deserve.

CHAPTER 4

Young pets -
How to
choose them

Young pets - How to choose them

Puppies, kittens, pot-bellied Vietnamese piglets - how do you choose what *species* to have, let alone what member of that species you want to join your household? Dogs remain the most popular pets, but cats are catching up fast. And after a few years in the doldrums, the number of pet birds is increasing again. Fish too are becoming more popular and small mammals such as guinea pigs and rats remain popular as children's pets. A cardinal rule to remember with all mammals is that females are usually easier to manage than males. (My wife keeps telling me that.) Lets look first at dogs.

A common reaction when trying to choose a pet, is to simply want to take them ALL home.

● Choosing the right dog

Choosing the right dog for you is a bit like choosing the right spouse; the only difference (at least for some of us) is that with dogs you repeat the exercise every ten to fifteen years. If you choose only by size and looks you might end up with the wrong dog in the wrong place and a misfit can make your life miserable. It can be destructive, aggressive, noisy and a downright nuisance to you and to your neighbours.

Emotion, of course, has a great deal to do with how we choose our new pups. But if we're willing to be practical there is a sensible series of questions we can first ask ourselves about how we live and what we want from our pets.

Start by making a list of both what you want from a dog and, equally important, what you can offer him. What type of housing do you live in? Do you have umpteen stairs and walls so thin that you always know what your neighbours are watching on television? If you do, then think twice about that cute little Dachshund you've always longed for. Dachshunds suffer from back problems and are robust barkers. In these circumstances a Dachs could prove to be a disastrous choice.

Do you have access to a garden, patio or back yard? Are there public open spaces nearby? I have a tiny back garden with only enough room for a large dog to do a three point turn but Hyde Park and Kensington Gardens are only minutes away. It means that I can provide an area where my two retrievers can spend time outside and attend to the calls of nature but I can also provide them with hundreds of acres of open space for the daily exercise that retrievers need.

Think about you and your family's future plans. Will you be willing or able to provide your dog with the exercise he needs? A Pekinese might be happy to chase slugs in a back garden the size of mine, but a terrier of similar size needs far more room. If you plan to keep active dogs you must also plan to make time available to exercise them. The age and activity level of the members of your household should be considered when selecting the perfect breed for you. Active people enjoy active dogs.

. . . .   Consider too the amount of money you want to spend on food and remember here that cost is not always directly related to size. Large breeds of dogs like Dobermanns, shepherds, setters and retrievers will eat almost anything. That means you can easily feed them

Poodles don't shed, although unfortunately they often suffer from the whims of their owners.

cheaper but just as nutritious dog foods than you can sometimes feed smaller breeds. Small breeds like Yorkies can be real faddy eaters. I know some that have made emotional blackmail into an art form - silky manipulators who have convinced their indulgent owners that unless they are fed only the best cuts of meat, fresh from the butcher, they will surely die of starvation. In those circumstances it can cost as much to feed a ten pound dog as it does to feed a thirty pounder in a more sensible manner.

Now add to your increasing list of requirements the type of coat, the size and the level of activity you want from your new pet. When considering the coat, think of how much time you will have available to groom it and how messy it will be when your dog moults. Our house is decorated in shades that are compatible with golden retriever hair and during the moulting seasons our vacuum cleaner takes up permanent residence in the living room. Owners of dogs with dark hair, such as black labradors and black cocker spaniels, have to contend with similar shedding problems and may not want to decorate their homes in black. If we were less willing to put up with semi-annual shedding, a non-shedding breed like a standard poodle would be a good choice.

Getting good advice on the behaviour of breeds is a tricky business. Your local library will probably have a good selection of books on specific breeds, but these are almost invariably written by people who are hopelessly addicted to their own breed. Quaint and gossipy they may be; in most instances they are biased and opinionated.

Neighbours, who usually have experience of the personalities of only a few breeds, are also biased. Pet shops can vary from terrible to excellent in the advice they give. Your local vet can almost always offer good and usually free advice. This is one of the few professional freebies that is still generally available to us. After all, we don't often get free advice from solicitors or architects or surveyors, but vets and their staff will still usually find the time to give you sensible information on what breed is most suitable for your circumstances.

The question of whether to get a mongrel or a pure bred dog is also filled with conflicting emotions. Almost invariably when you get a dog of mixed breeding there

. . . . is the satisfaction of knowing you are providing a home for an unwanted animal. The drawback is that it will be more difficult to predict your new pup's eventual size and, more important, its emotional state. The advantage of pure breds is that although there are always differences between individuals, certain breed characteristics apply to almost all members of a breed. German shepherds will be better guards than basset hounds. West Highland white terriers will bark more than Rottweilers. Irish setters will be more playful than bloodhounds.

The final decision to make before considering which specific breed is best for you and your family is whether to get a male or a female. Your previous experience will once more colour your decision but there are a few new statistical facts that are worth considering.

According to a recent and well-researched scientific paper, female dogs are better at obedience training, are easier to housetrain, and demand more affection. Male dogs are more playful, better at defending their territory, more destructive, have a higher level of general activity, are more aggressive towards other dogs and are more likely to try to dominate their owners. According to this survey there is no difference between the sexes in their watchdog barking, excess barking, excitability or likelihood of snapping at children. The nuisance of twice yearly seasons should not be a reason for avoiding bitches as pets. Early neutering eliminates that inconvenient aspect of keeping a bitch while at the same time ensuring that her personality remains as it is. Spaying at the wrong time - during a phantom pregnancy for example - can have an effect on behaviour but spaying at the right time does not.

Protection is one of the most common reasons for getting a dog, but there is no need to choose a potentially aggressive dog for this role. Most breeds, even soft sloppy ones such as Cavalier King Charles spaniels, can be trained to alert you to intruders by barking. The breeds that have been specifically developed

. . . . for guard and attack work, like German shepherds, Dobermanns and Rottweilers, should only be kept by families with a thorough understanding of how to control them.

When Liberty was spayed (and had head surgery at the same time), she was allowed - as the vet's dog - to recover from the anaesthetic in her own basket.

Having made your list of requirements, you should now be in a position to make a short list of breeds of dog that will suit you and your family. But how can you choose from over one hundred breeds, and how can you learn about the behaviour of each breed? There are two ways to do so.

The first is to take your list of requirements to your local vet, where you'll get first hand advice on which breeds are most suitable for you.

A good alternative is SELECTADOG, a computer generated scheme with details in its memory on the sixty most popular breeds of dog in Britain. SELECTADOG costs one pound, payable when you return a form they send you asking questions about where and how you live, the type of dog you like and what you want from your pet. The computer programme will reject incompatibilities. For example, if you indicate on the

. . . .

form that you want an active alert dog that will protect your property well and that you and your spouse both work, SELECTADOG will tell you that these are incompatible requirements - that active dogs need someone to be around. This scheme has been in operation in Britain for almost fifteen years although I suspect that few people know of its existence. It provides you with a description of the nature of breeds recommended for your lifestyle and a dog training chart. Similar related schemes are in operation elsewhere in Europe, in Norway, Sweden, Belgium, Holland and France for example so by now there is a good base of statistical information on which to base the computer program. The address is:

SELECTADOG, Pedigree Petfoods, PO Box 77, Burton-on-Trent DE 11 7BR

Finally, remember that as a breed increases in popularity the quality of that breed usually drops. That's because breeding ceases to be only in the hands of dedicated breeders and moves into the hands of 'puppy farmers', people who see only easy money in dog breeding. Always be wary of purchasing a new pup from anywhere other than a private home where you can see its mother, from a kennel or from a reputable pet shop.

It is true that pets often end up looking like their pet owners.

.... ● *Choosing the right cat*

At any given time there are probably over 200 million domestic cats living with people around the world. Seven million of them live in Britain and there are over 50 million more in the United States alone where the cat is now the most popular pet, outnumbering dogs. Cats make ideal companions. They are not as intrusive as dogs. They don't upset routine, are clean and relatively independent but still send us the signals we want to receive.

Cats are not as good at expressing their emotions with their faces as dogs are. Although they can move their whiskers and ears in a variety of ways they don't have the facial muscles that are necessary for the range of expressions that our dogs possess. We don't find it difficult to interpret when a cat is angry or frightened but otherwise all we usually see is a serene inscrutability, an expression of detached contentment that we find soothing and appealing.

The cat is our most recently domesticated animal. Whilst dogs were domesticated from wolves at least 12,000 and probably over 25,000 years ago the domestic cat emerged from wild obscurity only 3,000 to 4,000 years ago in Egypt and perhaps Mesopotamia. There is still today a healthy scientific argument concerning exactly what is a domestic cat. Because there is an indigenous wild cat in Scotland, it would seem logical that this species has had a dominant role to play in the evolution of cats like Milly. They certainly look similar. Facts however argue against the European wild cat being anything other than a marginal player in the evolution of the pet cat. Although both the European and North African wild cats possess similar tabby pattern coats, the North African cousin has a greater variety of coat colours and a greater affinity to humans. This last point can be proved by comparing the natural behaviour of the

European wild cat and the North African one. North African wild cats are easy to tame and *choose* to live near humans. The Scottish wild cat is impossible to tame and does everything it can to keep out of our way.

Because cats have so recently become our companions, and because until the last century we didn't intervene when it came to mating, their personalities and shapes don't vary anywhere near as much as dogs do. A Burmilla or a Devon Rex or even a blotched tabby today is simply the latest version of the original North African wild cat with four wheel drive, a superior paint job and nicer manners. And the original was and still is the best hunter that biological evolution ever produced.

It is important to remember this when choosing a cat as a companion. Right through to the very core of their beings, all cats are still hunters. In most of them their hunting abilities have been blunted through living with us, but their needs and their actions are still based on this basic drive. This is of course what makes them so appealing. It's why we could all sit for hours and simply watch Milly as a kitten do the most graceful and acrobatic four legged sideways pounce onto a ball of wool or a catnip mouse.

Dogs spend their lives on the ground, but a cat's world is vertical as well as horizontal - another important point to bear in mind when considering a cat as a companion. If your house is filled with Aunt Sally's prized collection of Belleek china, think twice about inviting a mountain-climbing moggie into your home.

Just as with dogs, where and how you live are important considerations in choosing a kitten. Can you let it outdoors? Do you *want* to let it outdoors? The statistics in London are certainly quite dramatic. Neutered, vaccinated indoor pet cats live an average of 15 years. Unneutered, unvaccinated outdoor cats live an average of less than two years. Traffic accidents are a major reason for the dramatic differences in life expectancy. If

. . . . you have a motorway at the bottom of your garden, be prepared for heartache if you allow your cat to roam freely. Indoor cats live longer but are more destructive. The only territory they have to mark is the sofa and the walls.

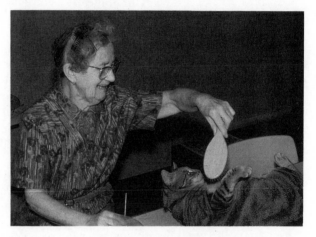

Cats can be amused by the simplest means.

Outdoor cats will find trees or posts to use as scratching posts, but indoor ones are restricted to the legs of the kitchen table or your best heavy curtains. One of the first things you should do when getting a kitten, is provide it with a purpose-made scratching post placed somewhere prominent. Milly was already using a rope-bound wood post at her breeder's and readily took to one of the same texture that we gave her at home. We didn't have a problem with her scratching other furniture, but if we did I would have armed myself with a good water pistol and blasted her each time her claws touched the untouchable object. The idea is to teach the kitten that unpleasant things happen when it does certain things, but not to make the discipline painful or excessive.

Cats are easier to run than dogs. Just as with dogs, kittens need primary vaccination and worming, then yearly check-ups, but their maintenance costs are lower. It shouldn't cost more than 50 pence a day to keep your cat well nourished.

One of the basic decisions to make in choosing a kitten is whether you want a short-haired or long-haired model. Short-haired cats need less grooming. Their raspy tongues are so good that they are virtually self-cleaning. Long-haired cats, on the other hand, need daily brushing. Their long hair is not proper heavy guard hair but rather the soft undercoat, the down, that has grown extra long. Every week I have to anaesthetize long-haired cats and shave them from stem to stern because their owners have allowed them to get so matted.

Milly is a long-haired cat, but with a difference. Maine Coons and Norwegian Forest Cats evolved in cold climates. They are the descendants of the survivors of cats from warmer climates, originally North Africa, taken up north. Those that had the warmest coats and were big enough to catch the local game, rabbits and hare, survived. The result is cats with long guard hair rather than long down. The hair doesn't tangle and needs brushing about once a week.

Although breed differences in size and behaviour are not as great in cats as in dogs, they should still be considered if you are choosing a pedigree cat. If I had the space, and fewer ornaments on the mantelpiece I'd like an Abyssinian or Somali cat. These are extroverts and clowns - bundles of energy that, if restricted to an indoor life, quickly learn that it's exciting to build up centrifugal speed on the ground and then do the wall of death. They are action cats that need exercise and attention.

Burmese and Siamese need just as much attention and are more vocal than most others. These breeds can be almost dog-like in their enjoyment of human companionship. Others, the Persians or long-hairs, can be remotely serene and almost ornament-like in their behaviour.

Detailed advice on breeds of kittens is available through the speciality cat magazines and the registering organizations whose addresses are given at the end of the book. Pedigrees still however only constitute 10% of our cats. The majority are moggies, infinitely cheaper (a rare pure bred can cost up to £500), just as varied in colours and just as enjoyable to have in your home.

Your local veterinary practice is the best place to start looking for a kitten. The nurses usually have a list of litters, but there is a seasonal fluctuation in their availability. Cats come into season more frequently as daylight hours increase, which means that the kittening season is primarily from March until August. That means that the likeliest times to find kittens ready to leave their mothers is from May until October.

For health reasons, breeders of pedigree cats usually keep their kittens until they are fully vaccinated at 12 weeks of age. The advantage is obvious. The disadvantage is that even by 12 weeks kittens are very set in their ways. Whilst dogs have very adaptable minds until they are three months old, the cat's socialization period ends sooner, at closer to two months. It can be advantageous to get your kitten at around nine weeks of age because by then he is no longer dependant upon his mother but he is still young enough to adapt well to his new environment, with dogs for example.

Choosing the sex of your cat is equally important. Male cats get into more fights than females, mark their territory with strongly scented urine and have an in-built desire to roam and protect a relatively large territory. Even neutered males will still want to have a decent-sized territory if given the opportunity. Females fight less, mark less and wander less, although they can still viciously defend their own territory, the back garden for example.

Neutering dramatically reduces the 'anti-social' behaviours of male cats and reduces but doesn't eliminate the wanderlust. When choosing a kitten, bear in mind that its natural urges might conflict with what you find acceptable behaviour. Some, if they've had the right mothers, become dexterous birders and will hunt incessantly. Others will share their gifts with you, presenting you at 6AM with frogs and slugs.

Just as dogs aren't humans in disguise, cats aren't dogs in disguise. They are still too close to their origins to act in any way other than that of their ancestors.

● *Choosing the right bird*

Do you want a pet that actually says 'Hello' when you come home or sings like Pavarotti? Birds are increasingly popular, especially with people whose lifestyles don't permit them to have dogs or cats, although I have strong reservations about keeping single birds in cages. The reason is that although we are superb dog substitutes and even pretty good cat substitutes we're quite miserable bird substitutes and can't really offer the activities that birds need. One budgie or parrot regurgitating seed for another shows sociability and affection. How many of us are willing to do that?

Budgies are the clowns of pet birds, the acrobats of millions of homes. These hardy little birds, if fed correctly, can even survive an English winter outdoors although Scotland might not suit them. They are gregarious animals, thriving on contact with other budgies, which is only logical when you consider that in Australia, where they come from, they are flocking birds. They make ideal pets for all ages, but especially the elderly as they are cheap to maintain and respond rewardingly to constant company and chat.

Mental stimulation is very important to budgies. Single birds will appear depressed if no one pays them any attention, although mirrors, bells and ladders help.

Budgies are clowns. Don't buy one with ruffled feathers that squats down lower than others.

The happiest, brightest birds are those that have other budgie companions and are allowed out of their cages.

Through selective breeding, budgies come in over 100 colours. Males have a blue cere (the area above the upper bill) whilst on females it is brown. It's important to know the difference since males are friendlier, more sociable and easier to finger tame and teach to talk.

When choosing a budgie look for an alert, sleek, clean and tidy bird. Don't buy a bird if its feathers are ruffled or if it seems to be squatting lower than the other birds. And the tamer it is when you buy it, the easier it

. . . .

will be to teach it to talk. The best age to buy a potential talker is six to eight weeks old.

To teach a budgie to talk simply repeat....and repeat.... and repeat. Women are better teachers for two reasons. They have more patience and, more important, they have higher pitched voices which budgies (and other talking birds) find easier to mimic.

Budgies cost more at Christmas because they naturally lay eggs in summer and so special sex cycle regulation is necessary to persuade them to produce winter broods.

Spring is the natural breeding season for canaries. They are more delicate than budgies, and perchers rather than climbers. They don't respond well to handling and should *not* be let loose from their cages as many tend to panic when allowed free flight.

Canaries have been with us for hundreds of years and have saved more human lives than any other bird. Their sensitivity to carbon monoxide led to their being used in mines to warn miners of danger: when the canary stopped singing it was time to leave the mine!

One of the recent changes I have seen in practice is the increasing numbers of large birds like parrots, macaws and cockatoos. These are expensive animals to purchase. Its not unusual to pay over £500 for a young healthy talking parrot. I know they have bird brains but I'm still amazed at how accurately they say the right thing at the right time. I have a Tymneh African Grey named Humphrey who now annoys us by mimicking a football whistle, a noise he picked up during the summer whilst listening to the World Cup. He also does such a perfect impression of Milly's meow that none of us can tell whether it's Humphrey or the cat.

I didn't choose Humphrey who was given to me by a client. But if I were to choose a large bird, I'd only choose

. . . .

one bred in Britain, even though these are the most expensive, for two reasons. The first reason concerns disease. Parrots can carry a serious disease called psittacosis, transmissible to us. British birds are very unlikely to carry it. Second, British birds haven't been captured in the wild. They are the descendants of other pet birds, bred and hand reared by their owners and tame as a result. They have been specifically bred as pet birds.

Humphrey chooses to spend most of his time in a large cage but he also perches on top of it or wings it through the living room to perch on the sash window at the front of the house and wolf whistle at passers-by (something I did NOT teach him). Birds can be unexpectedly amusing and, as research in 1986 showed, just watching them can lower your blood pressure. But so can other pets.

Humphrey, our grey parrot.

● *Choosing fish*

Watching fish cruising around in their tank lowers your blood pressure too. Goldfish are the cheapest to buy and to run but today the most popular area of fish-keeping is the tropical freshwater system. This is more expensive to set up, what with the tank, gravel, filter, air pump, heating, cover, lighting and plants, but once set up the running costs are minimal.

Fish are inexpensive pets, but setting up a tank can be costly.

Hardy fish such as neon tetras, guppies, platies and angel fish are the best to start with. It's important to take into account the natures of different species when choosing fish for your tank. When I was a university

. . . .

student I mistakenly added a pink cichlid to my existing tank of neon tetras, guppies, swordtails and angelfish. Soon only the angelfish remained. Swordfish can be bullies and angelfish can be quite carnivorous whereas guppies are prolific breeders and, if your tank is heavily planted with hiding places, can produce enough live young to survive.

When setting up a tank you can also take advantage of the fact that some fish prefer to inhabit different areas. Zebras and guppies like taking food from the surface whereas catfish are bottom feeders. Angelfish, mollies and tetras are midwater cruisers.

There can be a high mortality rate among tropical fish because of poor hygiene, but free advice is readily available. A booklet called *Fishkeeping Made Easy*, together with free further specific information is available from:
Aquarian Advisory Service
Oakwell Way
Birstall
Batley
West Yorkshire WF 17 9LU

● *Choosing other pets*

Keeping small mammals as pets is a twentieth century phenomenon. Until this century, some of these animals, like rabbits and guinea pigs, were simply a source of food or fur. Others, such as mice and rats, were viewed only as vermin, whilst hamsters and gerbils were only discovered quite recently.

Hamsters weren't discovered until 1930 when a litter of twelve babies was discovered at the end of an eight-foot burrow near Aleppo in Syria. Only three of these survived but fortunately two were females and four months later one of them gave birth. Every Syrian

. . . .   hamster in Britain today is a descendant from that litter! The first arrived here as laboratory animals in 1931.

Earlier in the century Chinese hamsters had arrived. These are much smaller than the more popular Syrian hamsters but it's only in the last six or seven years that I've started to see these animals at my surgery. These five-inch-long greyish brown bundles have a black stripe on their backs and whitish grey bellies. Through inbreeding they are now becoming less aggressive and quarrelsome which is why they're increasing in popularity.

Both Chinese and Syrian hamsters suffer from the disadvantage of being nocturnal animals. The disadvantage, I should add is ours, not theirs. 90% of their activity occurs after dark, and the racket they can make in a bedroom at midnight can sound like a pneumatic drill on tempered steel. It's best to house these animals where their night-time activity doesn't interfere with ours!

Their humorous bear-like looks and monkey-like acrobatics make hamsters obvious pets but even the more docile Syrian hamsters can give painful bites. Sticking a finger in a cage is asking for trouble. Chinese hamsters, because of their small size, are best housed in converted glass aquariums or in stacked hamster 'villages'. Syrian hamsters can also be housed in more standard metal cages. Avoid synthetic bedding for these pets. Fibres can wrap around their legs and cause gangrene. Instead, use wood shavings or shredded newspaper.

Hamsters will eat almost anything and are inveterate hoarders. They overstuff their cheek pouches so regularly that my nurses routinely check for stuck seeds or nuts before we go on to any other examination. Feed them seeds, grain, fruit and vegetables and when cleaning the cage, don't interfere with the stockpiled treasure trove unless its going off.

Don't be upset if you see your hamster eating his

droppings either. Its quite natural, as it is with rabbits, and an excellent source of vitamins B and K.

Gerbils arrived in Britain in 1964. These nocturnal 'desert rats' originated in the deserts of Mongolia. Coming from that environment they waste little water and so make clean and odourless pets.

Gerbils are magnificent excavators and are happiest and most fascinating when allowed to burrow. They are best housed in a converted aquarium at least thirty inches long and filled to a depth of about three inches with a mixture of Irish peat moss, seed compost and shredded straw. Make sure that the spout on the water bottle on the cage can't get covered when they burrow.

Gerbils enjoy many of the foods that hamsters eat but have a passion for sunflower seeds and raisins. Don't feed sunflower seeds alone though. They don't contain enough calcium for strong bones.

Although male hamsters make the gentlest pets (old female hamsters can become rather crotchety), female gerbils are usually easiest to handle. Males kept together will usually fight, often because we simply don't provide them with enough room, but females will live happily as pairs.

Gerbils are hardy creatures. The most common medical problem I have to treat is sore noses from burrowing in the wrong type of material. This is one reason why sand shouldn't be used in their cages.

Rabbits and guinea pigs have greater housing requirements than do hamsters and gerbils, for both thrive on living outdoors during the warm summer months. *Watership Down* has had a dramatic effect on our perception of rabbits. Until fairly recently rabbits were simply part of our diets, our clothing and our fairy tales. But now I frequently see free range house-bound rabbits, which have been litter box trained and so have access to the Wilton throughout the home. They're happiest hopping

. . . .

down a corridor and would seemingly be lost if put outdoors.

Rabbits thrive on companionship.

After dogs, cats, fish and birds, rabbits are our most popular pets. They range in size from a pound up to fifteen times that size and come in virtually all the colours of dogs and cats. Fancy breeds, lop ears and Angoras, have been created for showing but its usually best to stick to one of the dwarf breeds as a housepet. The British Rabbit Council, Pure Foy, 7 Kirkgate, Newark, Notts NG24 1AD can put you in touch with specialist breeders.

Rabbits are sociable and intelligent. They thrive on companionship, although bucks can be quite vicious in defending their territory or fighting over who services the doe. This is why does make the best pets, although I know of at least one buck rabbit who makes both a practical and interesting pet, ferociously guarding his owner's walled back garden against unwanted feline

. . . .   intruders. Big rabbits can slash viciously with their powerful hind legs.

Iindoor rabbits need more frequent attention to their teeth and nails, because they don't get normal exercise. Outdoor rabbits need shade in the summer and shelter in the winter. A dwarf breed needs at least four square feet of floor space in his hutch. Add a square foot of space for each additional pound in weight.

If you're providing an outdoor hutch, make sure it's raised off the ground to prevent rising damp and divide it into two sections, one for day-time use and one for sleeping. Wood chips or even cat litter makes good bedding but edible bedding such as straw is best. Water should be provided in bottles; water in dog bowls gets soiled with droppings.

If rabbits are allowed the freedom of the garden, remember they are good jumpers and burrowers. A two-foot fence is needed for dwarf rabbits and at least three feet for the larger breeders. Providing drain pipes to crawl through can help satisfy the need to burrow.

Rabbits and all other small mammals should be handled frequently from early in life. It makes them tamer and more manageable. Feed them commercial rabbit pellets supplemented with fruit and vegetables - cabbage, apples and carrots. Lettuce, incidentally, is one of the least nutritious foods you can feed.

Over the last several years there has been an increasing number of cases of myxomatosis, a virus disease of wild rabbits spread by fleas, in pet rabbits. The incidence varies throughout the country and your veterinary surgeon can advice you on the need for vaccination.

Guinea pigs are in many ways South American versions of rabbits. They're easy to manage, gentle creatures that enjoy being outdoors in the spring and summer but that don't have the protection against marauding cats that big

. . . .

buck rabbits have. That is why their hutches should at least ten inches high to prevent escaping, but also covered to prevent cats, foxes or dogs from entering.

Short-haired English varieties or wire-haired Abyssinians make the best pets. The long-haired Peruvian breeds are best left to the specialists. Guinea pigs thrive under the same conditions as rabbits - bedded on wood shavings, cat litter or preferably edible hay and kept in insulated hutches. Feed them pelleted guinea pig food and greens and, for a treat, parsley which they love. As with rabbits, their water should be supplied through a drinking bottle. Remember too that although rabbits have the image of being the most prolific species they have nothing on guinea pigs. These crafty little animals

A Victorian French circus performer.....

. . . .

are sexually mature at six weeks of age - and breed like, well, rabbits!

The children's pets that we have bred for longer than any others are the ones with the worst public image: mice and rats. Both have been bred for over a century and are still widely popular.

A serious drawback to mice is their smell. Mice use their urine, as dogs do, for social communication. This means that they urinate frequently and their bedding smells unless changed often, at the very least every other day.

Rats don't smell and make terrific pets. The image that they have - shifty, conniving and untrustworthy - is

...... who was clearly very attached to his rats.

. . . . unfair and probably based on their facial features and upon the fact that of all of these creatures the rat is by far the most intelligent. Rats can be friendly, humorous and sociable pets, easily recognizing their owners and showing affection to them. All pet rats are descended from the Norwegian rat and, as with mice, are usually white but come in a range of colours. 'Selfs' have a single body colour. 'Hooded' rats are not members of the Mafia but rather white animals with patches or stripes of colour. 'Marked' mice are the same.

Both mice and rats should be housed in metal or glass cages simply because they can so easily chew through wood or plastic. A cage twenty inches long, fifteen inches wide and ten inches high is suitable for one rat or two mice, and you should install climbing frames and exercise wheels, hollow tubes and ladders.

As with the other small mammals, wood shavings or shredded tissue makes good bedding and commercial pelleted food can be supplemented with dog biscuit and fruit. Rats in particular can be trained to do spectacular feats. On the TV series *The Mind Machine*, two years ago, rats were shown climbing a ladder to a platform, then pulling up the ladder so that they could reach the next platform. They were doing it for a food reward. If you plan to train your rat, use chocolate or cake as the reward, not cheese. Rats are true chocoholics.

To avoid population explosions, these animals too must be kept in single sex groups. Males will fight and are usually best kept singly.

There is a wide choice of pets for which we can provide a healthy, stimulating and safe environment. In return they can provide us with countless hours of learning, amusement and fun. Our responsibilities continue throughout their lives and this is what I will briefly discuss next.

CHAPTER 5

Responsibilities of pet keeping

Responsibilities of pet keeping

The responsibilities of pet keeping are obvious. We have a responsibility to keep our companion animals free from illness and disease and at the same time to make sure that they don't carry any diseases that are transmissible to humans. We have a responsibility to train them properly and to make sure they are well exercised. We have a responsibility to make sure they are properly identified in case they get lost, to groom them and to feed them nutritious and satisfying diets. We have a responsibility to control their breeding so that there is never a surplus of unwanted animals and we have a responsibility to have them properly cared for when we go on holiday. I would like to look at two of those responsibilities, feeding and training.

What should I feed my companion?

The question really falls into two parts. *How* should I feed my pet is just as important as *what* it should be fed. Every vet has his own ideas and here are mine.
There are three different ways to feed dogs and cats.

1

Have food permanently available, allowing your pet to eat when he feels like it.

2

Put down unlimited food but limit the time for feeding.

3

Supply a limited amount of food and expect your dog or cat to polish it all off.

Cats, always slightly more sensible than dogs, generally do rather well on free choice feeding, eating only what they need. Puppies, on the other hand, initially think they're in a foodie's Disneyland and will often play with the food they don't eat. The greatest drawback to free choice feeding is that bored cats and dogs with nothing much to do will often take up the offer of food because it's the most exciting pastime available. And don't forget that obesity is the most common nutritional disease in dogs and cats.

Restricting the time allowed for feeding is a half way measure. If you aren't sure you want to totally control feeding but don't want to leave eating completely to the whims of the animal you can put down what you consider to be a reasonable amount of food and then give your pet a specific amount of time to eat it. This is how I feed Milly, not because I want to but because, like many cats she likes to eat little and often. The problem is that two blond bombshells are always waiting in the wings to finish off what Milly doesn't immediately eat. (The dogs thank me daily for bringing a cat into their lives and thereby introducing them to cat food.) This method involves a little extra work in that you have to remove and store the uneaten food after the designated time.

Weaning kittens and pups begins at three weeks of age.

. . . .   Perhaps the most common method of feeding is to limit the amount of food you provide and to provide it as and when you see fit. This is how I feed Libby and Lex. They are fed twice daily, not because they need food twice daily (although scientific studies show that nutrients in the blood stream remain at more constant levels if you feed your pet this way) but because they find mealtimes exciting and feeding frequently reduces boredom.

My dogs are fed tinned food and biscuit. Liberty, who is spayed, is fed about one quarter fewer calories than Lexy who is not spayed. And when Lexy becomes (hopefully) pregnant next year her calorie intake will be increased even more. Several pet food manufacturers have recognized the need for foods with different energy levels and I'll have a good choice of high energy diets for her. There are also low calorie dog foods available for the less active or the downright slothful. unexpected advantages of these new high energy dry foods is that they produce less stool than conventional dog foods. And as more and more scoop laws are passed, this can be an important consideration in choosing your pet's diet. One of the great and unexpected advantages of these new high energy dry foods is that they produce less stool than conventional dog foods. And as more and more scoop laws are passed, this can be an important consideration in choosing your pet's diet. There are also low calorie dog foods available for the less active or downright slothful.

Cats are more fastidious eaters than dogs and enjoy variety more. Milly is only six months old, but as a young kitten I intentionally fed her a variety of nutritious foods so that I could determine where her tastes lay. A common old age problem in cats is kidney failure and the treatment for that is a dramatic reduction in protein in the diet. That means less meat and fish and more roughage and fat. I occasionally feed Milly spaghetti, chicken and rice and carrots as well as tinned and dry food, so that she acquires a taste for these foods now. That way I can switch her over to these less meaty foods

. . . . in the future if I need to. Right now she prefers tinned food, but her stools smell less when I feed her dry food.

I'm often asked whether it's possible or fair to feed dogs and cats vegetarian diets. The answer is that cats cannot survive without meat. Vegetable protein like soya cannot provide the essentials for life. Dogs, on the other hand, can survive on meat free diets as long as the diet is well balanced. It's a delicate art and sometimes unfair to impose upon what is primarily a meat-eating species.

I'm also asked whether dogs and cats should be given bones. Cats naturally eat the bones of the rodents and birds they catch and suffer no ill effects as a result. Calcium from bones is necessary for good health although all that a cat needs is already available in good commercial cat foods. But because cats are such fastidious eaters, it is exceptionally rare that any bones cause them problems. So unless you have a cat that wolfs down his meal, chewing bones is good for the teeth and gums.

Dogs have a different attitude to bones. They can become possessive over them and threaten even their closest friends if you try to remove them, and they eat bones too quickly. Never give a dog chop, chicken or rabbit bones. They're too brittle. If you must feed bones, give them beef shin or knuckle bones. And if you worry about mad cow disease make sure that you cook the bone well and remove all the marrow.

Don't indulge your pet. Don't let him treat your kitchen as if it were a restaurant. Don't offer a menu, offer a meal. All healthy pets will eat what is given them as long as it's fresh and appropriate for their species. If your pet becomes fussy about his eating you should visit your vet. Always have fresh water available. If you notice that your pet is drinking more than he normally does, that also calls for a visit to your vet. Increased thirst is a clinical sign of many diseases, some of which are serious.

● *Teaching commands*

It's easy to teach cats commands. Just observe what they do then ask them to do it. Fortunately cats come already housetrained and will use a litter tray if one is provided. The feel and the smell of the litter is important and you might find that if you suddenly change the type of litter you use, your cat might stop using the tray.

Housetraining a pup follows simple rules. No punishment - only praise. Take him to relieve himself on newspaper when he wakes up, after he eats and after playing. Once he uses the newspaper, reduce the quantity of it on the floor and gradually move his paper closer to your back door. Each time he 'performs' use a particular phrase like 'hurry up'. And in a short time all you need to give is the command and he will relieve himself. (Incidentally, this is how elephants are trained to relieve themselves before they enter the circus ring.)

Aggression is the most common behaviour problem in dogs.

Teaching any commands to your dog should be fun for you and also for him. But, don't let your democratic ideals get in the way of proper training. These aren't party tricks you are teaching. They are the basis for a successful and satisfying relationship. A dog enjoys following instructions and is happy and contented to obey your commands.

Training begins as soon as you get your pup, as early as seven to eight weeks of age. Get him used to wearing a collar - a flat or rolled leather one is often best. Use a simple word to release him from his commands. The simplest release word to teach is 'OK'. And, of course, the best negative word is 'NO'.

Teach both verbal and visual commands at the same time. Never 'ask' your dog to do something. Don't issue requests with question mark endings. Always use commands that are given fairly and with confidence.

● *Sit*

1

Start training on the first day you have your pup.

2

Let him first sniff his food in his bowl. Then, each time he is fed hold his bowl above his head in such a way that he is most likely to sit down to keep his eyes on it. Say 'SIT' while he does so.

3

If he doesn't sit on his own, use your hand and gently push his rump down.

4

Reward him for sitting by giving him his meal.

The command to 'SIT' should not always be coupled with a food reward. Carry out this same simple training three or four times daily, when there are no distractions, by offering praise as his reward:

1

Go to a quiet area and hold a toy or simply snap your fingers above your pup's head while at the same time commanding him to 'SIT'.

. . . .

2

When he does so calmly reward him with praise. Don't wind him up with excitement because if he is too excited he will lose his attention.

3

Release him from his 'SIT' position by saying 'OK' and always finish off a training session with praise and activity.

4

Once he has learned to 'SIT' in quiet surroundings, move to different areas including indoors and outdoors so that he learns to obey command in different situations.

● *Stay*

Once more start training indoors in a quiet place where there are no distractions. Your pup is more likely to obey if he wears his collar and lead. In that way you retain control over him. Remember, he won't have the foggiest idea what 'STAY' means when you first use the command. Never discipline him during training for disobeying. Simply go back to the previous stage and repeat the exercise.

1

Crouch down and tell your pup to 'SIT' and when he does so then tell him to 'STAY'.

2

Use a flat tone of voice and while issuing your command turn the palm of your hand towards your pup and move it towards him until it almost touches his nose.

. . . .

3

Stand up, keeping the palm of your hand near his nose, then draw back while maintaining your hand's visual impact.

4

After a few seconds release him from his 'STAY' by saying 'OK'.

Needless to say he won't obey at first because he won't know what you're trying to do. Don't get angry with him and don't think he's stupid either. Remember, he's just starting to learn. Firmly but patiently say 'NO' when he moves, walk him back, tell him to 'SIT', and repeat the steps I've just outlined.

He might find it difficult to understand that you simply want him to 'SIT' and might lie down instead. If you let him do so you're teaching him a faulty command. He should only sit when you command him to 'SIT'. If he lies down, do the following.

1

Tell him 'NO' when he lies down and this time, using slight tension on his lead, repeat the commands to 'SIT' and 'STAY'.

2

If he breaks your command by lying down, be patient and repeat the series once more.

3

If he is obviously flagging, remember to always finish training on a positive note and finish off with a command you know he will obey, 'SIT'.

. . . .

4

Once he will 'SIT' and 'STAY' on command with you standing near him, gradually begin to get farther away from him until he is willing to obey when you are standing at the farthest end of his lead. Always use the lead during training. That way you are assured of having your dog under your ultimate control.

5

As he comes to understand the meaning of the word 'STAY' lengthen the time he will stay but do so erratically. Command him to stay for a minute, for 30 seconds, for two minutes. Be unpredictable in the duration of the command.

6

Once he is well trained in a quiet setting, move to a more stimulating environment such as the garden or the street.

7

If he backslides in his training return to the previous success level and always remember to finish training on a positive note.

● Come

All pups will willingly come to their owners but just because they will as pups doesn't mean they will as adults. Training should start as soon as your new pup arrives in your home but must be reinforced, especially as dogs mature.

. . . . **1**

Put your pup down, move a few feet away from him then wave your arms and call him by name by saying 'BENJIE! COME'. He will almost instinctively do so.

2

Reward him with affection or even a food reward such as a vitamin tablet.

3

Continue to train in this way, using his lead if necessary, until he reliably comes to you each time he is called.

4

Once he is well trained in a quiet environment, move into a more stimulating one outdoors and repeat the same series of commands but use his lead so that there is no possibility of disobeying.

5

When he fluently obeys your command to 'COME' to his name while he is at the end of his lead, graduate to the same command without the safety of his lead.

6

Never train your pup to 'COME' to command to something that he dislikes, like discipline, or a bath. Let me repeat this rule because it is so important. NEVER CALL YOUR DOG TO PUNISH HIM. If punishment is due, go to him rather than have him come to you.

In most instances you will find the command to 'COME' an easy one to teach, until your dog reaches sexual maturity. That's when the pliable pup becomes a stubborn teenager. He will need firm handling if you want him to continue to obey this command. This is when he will *really* be learning to obey the command to 'COME' rather than simply following his urge to be with you.

1

Using your lead to assure control, command your dog to 'SIT'and 'STAY'.

2

Move six feet away from him and using his name, command, 'BENJIE. COME'.

3

Open your arms to him or in any other way stimulate him to come to you.

4

Praise him with touch or sometimes with a titbit of food.

5

Continue this routine but alter the sequence of commands. Tell him for example, to 'SIT' when he nears you.

6

Repeat this series of commands in all variations so that your dog does not become used to a specific series of commands. Once this has been done, proceed to issue commands when he is off his lead.

7

If he does not obey off his lead, revert to his previous successful level of training; command him to 'SIT' and 'STAY', go to him, put his lead on and saying 'COME' repeatedly, walk him to where you were previously standing. Both of you will find this immensely boring but follow up with a few 'SIT-STAY' commands at that site.

8

Always praise your dog when he comes. Use the same words such as 'Good dog!' or 'Good Benjie!' and a positive tone of voice, different to your voice of displeasure.

9

Once more, always finish training on a high note, even if you secretly want to strangle your dog because he's been concentrating on a fluffy young Poodle rather than on your commands. If he has been wilfully disobedient to your command to 'COME', finish off training with 'SIT', 'STAY' and a reward from you for his doing so. But keep the reward perfunctory.

● *Down*

This is an important command for two reasons. First of all, it teaches your dog to drop on command wherever he is. If he's chasing a squirrel out onto the street this could save his life. But, equally important, dropping down is a sign of subservience in dogs and training your dog to obey the command 'DOWN' is an effective way of showing your dominance over him. Teaching the command 'DOWN' reinforces your position as leader of the pack and teaches your dog to be calm. Dominant

. . . .   dogs should be commanded to stay 'DOWN' several times each day and for at least fifteen minutes at a time!

1

Command your pup to 'SIT'.

2

Pat the floor and command your pup 'DOWN'. If you pat directly under him he might lie down simply to sniff your hand.

3

Praise your pup if he obeys your command.

4

If he does not obey, gently draw his forelegs forward while repeating the command, 'DOWN' and then reward him with stroking and verbal praise.

5

Once he is comfortably down, command him to 'STAY' and praise him for doing so.

6

Get up, back away, then say 'OK' to release him from the command.

7

Don't rush things. Carry out this procedure only a few times a day to begin with.

Fish are increasingly popular as pets. This is a good thing, for simply watching fish swimming in a tank lowers your blood pressure.

Above, brushing teeth helps preserve gums.

Left, most dogs need active daily excercise.

Below, many cats are contented to lead indoor lives.

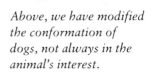

Above, we have modified the conformation of dogs, not always in the animal's interest.

Left, top and bottom, dogs are magnificent at training their families to include them in their activities.

Right, budgies are sociable birds and are best kept in pairs.

Below, our image of the cat is not distinct. We admire his grace and elegance, but one out of four people don't trust him.

8

Add the 'DOWN' and 'DOWN-STAY' commands to the repertoire of 'SIT', 'STAY' and 'COME' commands that your pup has already learned.

9

Once this command is obeyed indoors off his lead, move outdoors to a more stimulating environment and repeat the training procedure initially with his lead on.

10

Don't release him from a 'DOWN-STAY' simply because he looks restless.

11

Always reinforce training. Whenever you are out with your dog mix and match the commands 'SIT', 'STAY', 'COME' and 'DOWN'. Do so randomly so that he must constantly be thinking about what you are telling him to do. In that way he will always look upon you as his leader. He will respect you, and you in turn will have the positive influence on him that will make him a delightful, responsive and intelligent companion.

.... **● *Behaviour problems***

If a behaviour problem develops with your dog or cat it's best to discuss it first with your veterinarian. Once the problem has been analysed, you will need to retrain your pet. The first type of retraining applies only to dogs and involves training him to do something else instead of acting in his objectionable way.

1

Identify the specific circumstances of the situation in which your dog acts objectionably. For example, if he barks when someone comes to your door, does he do so for everyone or just when certain people arrive?

2

Decide upon a behaviour that you want your dog to do rather than the one he is doing. For example, if he barks when visitors arrive you might want him to hold a toy in his mouth instead.

3

Train him to perform the new behaviour on command and reinforce this new behaviour with a powerful reward (food). Do this initially every time he carries out the behaviour and then intermittently.

4

Under controlled circumstances create the situation that initially caused his unacceptable behaviour (such as someone coming to the door). Before the dog reacts (by pricking up his ears) immediately get his attention and have him carry out his new behaviour. Reward him for obeying.

5

Keep training him this way by increasing the intensity of what used to make him behave badly until he behaves properly when under normal uncontrolled conditions.

The second method of retraining can be used with both dogs and cats. Pets are exposed to a situation that has, for example, frightened them, and learn through desensitizing, not to be frightened.

1

The objective is to stop a cat or dog from responding in an unacceptable way in a particular situation. For example if a dog or cat has developed a fear of certain noises the objective is to make those noises less fearful. Simply because dogs can be so easily trained compared to cats this type of training is more successful with them. Certain parts apply only to dogs.

2

Identify the specific circumstances that elicit the unacceptable response and make sure that you can control these circumstances. For example, if your pet has a fear of loud noises it is best to use a recording of them instead so that you can control the intensity.

3

Make sure that your controlled stimulus (eg recording) actually does provoke your pet to act in his acceptable way when it is used to full intensity.

. . . .

4

Introduce the stimulus at its lowest intensity and reward your pet for quiet behaviour. (If retraining a dog, first train him to lie down on command for at least fifteen minutes. This is best done under highly controlled circumstances such as on a specific rug. Initially reward his behaviour with simple food rewards given every fifteen or twenty seconds at first, then gradually at greater intervals.)

5

Over a period of days and weeks, gradually increase the intensity of the stimulus, always rewarding quiet behaviour.

6

If at any time your pet shows objectionable behaviour stop the training at a previous level where he behaved acceptably. Always finish a training session on a positive note.

To be a responsible pet owner isn't difficult. All it takes is a little common sense. Here are some simple ideas to follow.

1

Make sure your pet carries his identity papers. A collar and tag works best but tattoos and 'identichips' are also valuable.

2

Worm your dog or cat regularly with one of the new wormers available from your vet.

. . . .

3

Don't let your pet foul buildings, pavements, lawns, gardens or open spaces where children play. If he accidently does so clean up after him.

4

Keep your dog on a lead near roads or near farm animals.

5

Don't allow your dog to bark and disturb your neighbours.

6

Provide your pet with his own bed, bedding and dishes.

7

Keep your pet free from parasites such as fleas, and groom him regularly.

Make sure that your controlled stimulus (eg recording) actually does provoke your pet to act in his unacceptable way when it is used at full intensity.

8

Make proper kennel arrangements before you go on holiday.

9

Control the pet population explosion by getting appropriate advice from your vet.

10

Don't assume that *all* people enjoy the company of animals as much as you.

Above all else *stimulate* your pets. They are completely dependant upon us for physical exercise and for their mental stimulation - the subject I will discuss next.

CHAPTER 6

Mature pets-
How to
amuse them

Mature pets - How to amuse them

There is a simple rule to follow if we are to keep animals successfully as pets. ALL PETS NEED MENTAL STIMULATION. It doesn't matter whether they swim, fly or walk, they all need their brains stimulated just as much as they need their bodies exercised. Fish should be given the opportunity to find their food and to investigate exciting environments. Birds should be able to indulge in mutual grooming and opening nuts and seeds. Small mammals should be provided with tunnels and wheels and materials to excavate. All of them need to use their minds as well as their bodies.

Pets and children need to use their minds as well as their bodies

The more intelligent the pet is, the more necessary it is to be sure that you provide him with adequate mental stimulation. As dogs and cats are our most intelligent pets, these are the species that require the most attention from us. We might be providing them with all the

. . . . necessities to live long and healthy lives, but in many instances these are being provided from within the confines of a luxurious jail.

Fortunately, most of our dogs and cats are supremely contented to live out their lives in such safe and cosy surroundings. Most are content to have *us* do all the hunting for them whilst they put their feet up on the sofa and relax in front of the fire. I often tell cat owners that they should feed their cats some meat on the bone so that their pets use their teeth and gums in a natural way to delay the onset of gum disease. Have you ever tried convincing a cat to work harder for something? Once he knows that his meal comes mixed, tasty and free of skin and bone he's unlikely to accede to your demands that he revert to a more 'natural' type of eating.

The dog's desire to gnaw is more constant but even so it can be difficult to convince a dog to change his ways once he is mature. Once more, this is a problem with regard to gum disease in dogs. Most, especially the little ones, deeply resent their owners trying to brush their teeth, but this is the only way to slow down the almost inevitable gum disease that most dogs get with age. The easiest way to overcome the problem is to start brushing your dog's teeth when he is still a pup so that it becomes part of his routine, rather than wait until it becomes a necessity.

Bored dogs and cats are destructive pets. Cats that don't go outdoors have extra energy to burn and use it up doing a Grand Prix circuit through the house. Dogs that are left alone vent their frustration by eating the walls, digging and chewing up the carpets or, when overwhelmingly anxious, by urinating and defecating indoors. Boredom can be alleviated if we are willing to act as dog and cat substitutes for our pets, to actively play with them and stimulate their minds.

Milly's mind is stimulated by provoking her natural

. . . .   hunting instincts. She's learned that Humphrey the parrot is out of bounds (although her eyes still dilate when he flaps his wings) but is allowed in the back garden to listen to the sounds, smell the odours (especially the odour of the nearby kebab house) and watch the activity in the trees. She's allowed to investigate the plant beds and climb the trees but she's always monitored as I haven't spayed her and when she comes into season her natural inclination will be to wander. After she has had a litter, and been spayed she'll be more contented to stay in the security of her back garden.

Indoors we actively play with her with cat toys. Small styrofoam balls wound with wool are perfect cheap and stimulating toys for cats. Similarly, lightweight toys that move in a lolloping manner are more stimulating than those that just roll. Milly is much more fascinated by movement that she can't predict than by uniform movement.

The fun of play goes both ways. We of course enjoy seeing her play. It's fun to see how her mind is working. She in turn is stimulated by the activity and gets to use her keen senses. Playing games is fun for pets because it is a break from routine. It's fun for us too because it brings out the child in us and we all need to escape from the pressures of work and worry. We need what the psychologists call 'down time' time when both our mental and physical activity are not 'responsibility' oriented but rather are directed towards the trivial and the mundane, like playing with the cat.

Because of his more gregarious behaviour, a dog can be played with in many more exciting ways, all of which provide him with mental stimulation. And teaching your dog to play games is simple as long as you remember that teaching should be fun and playing should be fun. In that way both you and your dog get equal rewards.

My children play 'hide and seek' with Lib and Lex. We all go to the park and, whilst one child distracts the dogs, the other hides behind a tree. They are then instructed to 'Find Ben!' and with gazelle-like hops and ears as high as a German shepherds they go searching, scenting the air and listening for any sounds that will give them clues where Ben has hidden. They also play with each other. They hare off after each other, frequently alternating which one is actually doing the chasing. This alone is reason enough to have two dogs, for who makes a better playmate for a dog than another dog.

Hide and seek is a simple game to play and I guarantee you will feel refreshingly foolish and childlike if you do. You can play it indoors too, but on rainy days, playing 'seek and find' can be more fun.

Play stimulates hunting behaviour in kittens.

In this game the dog is shown a favourite toy and at the beginning of training it is hidden where he can easily find it. When he does so, he's rewarded with good words and pats. As the teaching progresses, the hiding places become more difficult until finally you reach the stage where your dog is invited to leave the room while his toy is hidden and he's then invited back in to find it. If you use something with a smell that dogs find easy to detect, like a rubber ring, he will have no difficulty finding the hidden treasure. The game gives him the chance to think and to use his senses.

Of all the games to teach your dog, the most enduring and variable is 'retrieve'. It can be played on land or on water. Retrievable objects can be tennis balls or sticks. My dogs prefer Frisbees and Aerobees and, as natural born retrievers, excel at the game.

Any dog can be taught to retrieve, the only qualification being that they are healthy dogs in good physical condition. Only young healthy dogs should play Frisbee as it requires strong hind legs in particular and overweight dogs run the risk of damaging ligaments behind their knees. If you're going to use a Frisbee be sure that its a light taper edged model. Sharper models and Aerobees, even though the latter have soft edges, can still damage your dog's mouth.

Dogs are possessive. They always want what another dog has, so first tease your dog a little to get him interested in the Frisbee. Games are meant to be fun so be enthusiastic. If he still isn't interested, roll it on the ground. Act like a fool. Make him think it's your most precious possession. If he's still not interested he's either brain dead or a Bloodhound. Not all breeds will respond but most will.

Once he's interested, teach him to release the Frisbee when you say 'give'. Do this by pulling up his upper lips behind his nose to release the object. Reward him with a little affection or a titbit of food. I taught Lib and Lex to release by taking the object and then rewarding them by giving it straight back.

When your dog has learned to 'give', you can increase his enthusiasm for the Frisbee by playing tug of war with it although you should never play tug of war games with dogs you want to have soft mouths or with potentially dominant dogs. (They want to win too badly.) Some dogs are real show offs and will rapidly progress from retrieving throws to retrieving skips and bounces. They'll learn to read throws accurately and can soon be better than you are at the game. To avoid sore pads and hard landings always play games like this on grass or sand. And be sure to have some water on hand. Frisbee retrieving can be hard work.

When I was young, people let their pets stay out all night. Today we have a greater responsibility for our pets. Dogs in particular should never be allowed to wander. It's not in their interest and because of the problems they can create, it's antisocial on our part to let them do so. That's why it's so important for them to have their mental activity provided by us. And throwing off your inhibitions is good for you too. Mental stimulation is important throughout your pet's life. If they continue to be mentally stimulated when they grow old their senior years will be healthier, more active and more enjoyable.

● *Golden oldies*

The signs of old age in pets are similar to the signs of old age in us. Older pets have poorer reflexes and suffer memory losses. The reason why this happens is quite simple. When a pet is in his prime, messages pass up and down his nerves at around 225 miles per hour. That's why his responses can be so amazingly fast. But in the elderly pet, messages slow down to perhaps 50 miles per hour.

. . . .

Something else happens too. Inside the brain of the young pet the nerve cells fire off chemical messages to each other with machine gun rapidity. One single nerve cell in the brain might have connections with up to 10,000 other cells. As the pet gets older however many of these cells lose thousands of their connections. The result is that the older pet needs more time to react - more time to work things out.

This is important to understand because it means that the old adage, 'You can't teach an old pet new tricks' is wrong.

You *can* teach an old pet new tricks as long as you understand that his brain will take a lot longer to process the information you are giving it.

Liberty retrieving her Aerobee.

My previous dog, Honey, a golden retriever, lived to nearly seventeen years of age and was a classic example of both the elderly dog's ability to learn new tricks but also of the irreversibility of some senile changes. When Honey was about fourteen years old she went deaf. She developed arthritis of the bones in her ears. This meant that we could no longer give her verbal commands, to SIT or STAY for example. But with a speed that amazed me she very rapidly learned sign language. She was taught that showing her the palm of my hand, fingers up, meant STAY or that my pointing with a finger to the ground meant LIE DOWN.

. . . . Just as with other dogs her age Honey experienced other old age changes that affected her behaviour. The brain is a beehive of chemical activity throughout life and needs an amazing amount of nourishment in order to perform properly. That's why over 20% of the blood that is pumped out of the heart goes straight to the brain.

With old age however, blood vessels lose their elasticity and the lungs become less efficient in taking in oxygen. Complicating matters even more, tiny little microscopic haemorrhages can occur in blood vessels in the brain itself. One consequence of all of this is that older dogs can become irritable if they are disturbed, can become slower at obeying commands and can eventually revert in many ways to a puppy-like dependence upon us.

The good news is that scientists have recently discovered that there are many ways in which we can delay these inevitable changes. A good example is scent.

The ability to smell things is one of the first senses that a pup develops and one of the last that the elderly dog loses. And the more he uses his nose the longer he'll be good at using it.

From other experiments, we also know that increasing the supply of oxygen to the brain in old dogs improves long term memory quite dramatically. What that means is that the other old adage, 'Let sleeping dogs lie' should be changed too. Let sleeping dogs lie, but get them up and make sure they get routine exercise too. Get their lungs going so that they can take in oxygen and feed their minds with it.

One of the most exciting research conclusions recently showed that even in old age animals have the ability to improve how their brains work. Old pets have smaller brains than young pets. The cause is simply shrinkage. But with activity and mental stimulation, that shrinkage can be reversed.

. . . .

Pensive stone dog in Highgate cemetary.

Although there is a genetic biological clock that has programmed the ultimate life span of each of our pets, there are also influences from the environment that we can control and improve. We can alter the decay of memory by providing our pets with mental stimulation.If we stimulate their minds we can alter the ageing process and make life more interesting for them in their latter years. The brain is built on instructions from genes but is then modified by events throughout life. Even the ultimate behaviour changes of ageing can be altered by improving our pet's environment. The cycle of life is inevitable however and the time comes when we must make a decision over whether the quality of our pet's life is up to a minimum standard,

There are no fixed rules on how to make the decision to euthanise a pet but there can be guidelines. When your elderly pet is ill or simply going 'downhill' these are some of the questions to ask.

1

Is the condition prolonged, recurring or getting worse?

2

Is the condition no longer responding to treatment?

3

Is he suffering either physically or mentally?

4

Is it no longer possible to alleviate that pain or suffering?

5

If he should recover, is he likely to be chronically ill, an invalid or unable to care for himself?

6

If he recovers is he likely to no longer be able to enjoy life or will he have severe personality changes?

If the answers to all of these questions is 'yes' then your decision is obvious. But if the answer to three or four of these questions is 'no' then you should ask yourself these questions.

1

Can I provide the necessary care?

2

Will this care seriously interfere with my own or my family's life?

3

Will the cost be unbearably expensive?

Remember, there is a difference between living and being kept alive. The quality of your pet's life is the most important fact.

There are many reasons for euthanasia and these include:

1

Overwhelming physical injury.

2

Irreversible disease that has progressed beyond a point where distress or discomfort can be controlled

3

Old age 'wear and tear' affecting the quality of life.

. . . . **4**

Physical injury, disease or wear and tear resulting in permanent loss of control of body functions.

5

Aggressiveness with danger to owner or others.

6

Pet carries disease dangerous to humans

We have developed a whole spectrum of social and religious customs to help people to grieve when a fellow human dies. Barriers often come down and for a period after a death there can be increased communication for those who are grieving with more conversation, more communication and more touching. But many of us don't know what to do when a pet dies. Is it morally right to grieve deeply over the death of an animal? Is it right to feel such deep emotion, in some people deeper than the grief they felt when a relative died? Is it right to show such grief? These are questions that many veterinarians have pondered over, for euthanasia is one of the most difficult parts of practice. Of course it's right to feel such pain. A pet has been a member of the family and has been treated as a child. If you pretend you don't feel as badly as you do or, even worse, feel guilty about how dreadful you feel you will only be storing up emotional problems for the future.

The bond we develop with our pets is often stronger that we might suppose, sometimes the strongest we have with any living thing. In a survey reported by the American magazine *Psychology Today*, one of the largest surveys of pet owners ever undertaken, 90% said that their pets were very important to them, 88% said that stroking their pets helped them to relax, 87% considered their pets to be members of the family and 75% said that their pets increased the fun of family life. Other surveys in both the United States and here in

. . . . Britain show that half of all dog and cat owners keep pictures of their pets in their wallets or on their walls. Half of us say that our pets make us feel more secure and half of us allow our pets to sleep with a member of the family. Most compelling and perhaps even tragic in its own way is the fact that 79% of the people in the *Psychology Today* survey said that at some time their pet has been their closest companion.

Because the relationship we have with our pets can be so intense, the grief that is experienced when they die can be overwhelming. 75% of pet owners, according to surveys, have experienced difficulties or disruption of their lives after a pet died. One third had to take time off work and an equal number experienced difficulties in their relationships with other people. We humans can only think in human terms and once we have made an emotional investment in a pet we pay the consequences in the grief we feel when that pet dies. That most of us overcome our grief is shown by the fact that within a year of the death of a pet, 75% of pet owners have introduced a new pet into their homes.

Pets enrich our lives. They remind us that we are part of a living world and of our responsibilities to that world. Pets are a window through which we can view nature and marvel at how varied and wonderful it is. In their own curious and subliminal way, their presence makes life more interesting, more fascinating, more secure and more rewarding. People all over the world, of different cultural and economic backgrounds keep pets. They do so not for any material reward but simply because they enjoy it. Sharing is fun.

Useful addresses

The charity most concerned with the relationship between people and pets is:

SOCIETY FOR COMPANION ANIMAL STUDIES
7 Botanic Mews Lane
Glasgow G20 SAA

Charities that train or provide service dogs include:

HEARING DOGS FOR THE DEAF
Little Close
Lower Icknield Way
Lewknor
Oxford OX9 5RY

GUIDE DOGS FOR THE BLIND
Alexander House
9 Park Street
Windsor
Berks SL4 1JR

PAT DOGS
Rocky Bank
4 New Road
Ditton
Kent ME20 7AD

PET FOSTERING SERVICE SCOTLAND
PO Box 12
Montrose DD10 8YD

Companion animal welfare groups include:

RSPCA
The Causeway
Horsham
West Sussex RH12 1HG

USPCA
11 Drumview Road
Ballymagarrick
Lisburn
Northern Ireland BT27 6YF

SSPCA
19 Melville Street
Edinburgh
Scotland EH3 7PL

NATIONAL CANINE DEFENCE LEAGUE
1/2 Pratt Mews
London NW1 0AD

WOOD GREEN ANIMAL SHELTERS
Highway Cottage
Chiswell Road
Heydon
Royston
Herts SG8 8BR

PEOPLE'S DISPENSARY FOR SICK ANIMALS
PDSA House
South Street
Dorking
Surrey RH4 3LB

BLUE CROSS
1 Hugh Street
London SW1V 1QQ

BATTERSEA DOGS' HOME
4 Battersea Park Road
London SW8 4AA

CATS' PROTECTION LEAGUE
17 Kings Road
Horsham
West Sussex RH13 5PP

Registering organizations for dogs and cats are:

GOVERNING COUNCIL OF THE CAT FANCY
26 Essex Road
Enfield
Middlesex

CAT ASSOCIATION OF BRITAIN
Hunting Grove
Lowfield Heath
Crawley
West Sussex RH11)py

THE KENNEL CLUB
1 Clarges Street
London W1Y 8AB

Organizations involved in research in the diseases of companion animals and in their relationship with us include:

ANIMAL HEALTH TRUST
Lanwades Hall
Newmarket
Suffolk CB8 7PN

BSAVA CLINICAL STUDIES TRUST FUND
5 St George's Terrace
Cheltenham
Glos GL50 3PT

The governing and scientific bodies of the veterinary profession are:

ROYAL COLLEGE OF VETERINARY SURGEONS
32 Belgrave Square
London SW1X 8QP

BRITISH VETERINARY ASSOCIATION
7 Mansfield Street
London W1m 0AT

BRITISH SMALL ANIMAL VETERINARY ASSOCIATION
5 St George's Terrace
Cheltenham
Glos. GL50 3PT

BRITISH VETERINARY NURSES ASSOCIATION
The Seedbed Centre
Coldharbour Road
Harlow
Essex CM19 5AF

Several specialist magazines and newspapers are written for pet owners. They include:

CAT WORLD
10 Western World
Shoreham by Sea
West Sussex BN4 5WD

CATS
5 James Leigh Street
Manchester M1 6EX

DOG WORLD
9 Tufton Street
Ashford
Kent TN23 1QN

OUR DOGS
5 Oxford Road
Station Approach
Manchester M60 15X

Other organizations involved with companion animals include:

THE PET HEALTH COUNCIL
4 Bedford Square
London WC2B 3RA

PET FOOD MANUFACTURERS ASSOCIATION
6 Catherine Street
London WC2B

FELINE ADVISORY BUREAU
350 Upper Richmond Road
London SW15 6TL